"I can read. I feel alive now."

Devin C,
First time reader
26

TESTIMONIALS
PROFESSIONALS:

"When Marilee and Judy shared their teaching strategies with me, I responded, "You have a moral obligation to share this with other children." I knew this book was important for everyone when I saw the results of the strategies described. To put it simply, it works! With over 30 years of searching for "programs" to help students learn to read, I have learned that teaching this code arms them with the skills necessary to be a reader for the rest of their lives."

Sharon B.,
Assistant Superintendent (retired)
School District of Lee County, FL

I have been using Raising Robust Readers with a young student with Down syndrome from the United Arab Emirates who is also an ESL learner. It has been amazing to see his quick progress during a very short time! The creative, research-based materials combined with the program's flexibility made it a perfect fit for him.

Noemi H.,
Special Education Teacher

"Wow, you have distilled, into one easy-to-read-and-understand article, years of study on my part... It's all so very different from how I was trained as a classroom teacher and reading specialist. I got my master's in reading so I could teach anyone to read. And here I am fourteen years later, still learning... This is a fabulous resource—thank you!"

Jennifer N.,
Master's Degree Reading

"I am amazed how yours is the first program in all my years as an elementary teacher and furthermore as a homeschooling parent, that truly dispels the myth of understanding syllables and how to attack them in attempting to read and decode words. I think that there are so many students whose literacy issues could be healed if only they had your program. And let me also add that the way your program has been developed has left no stone unturned. The minute I think of something that I think has been missed, I am quickly corrected by seeing the unique way in which you have considered all the nuances of the English language!...Children need not toil and suffer through learning to read..."

Stacey C.,
Elementary Teacher

"As I underline the multi-letter phonograms for this week's spelling words, I shudder to think that I ever taught spelling without doing so. My enthusiasm comes from my realization that I am developing skills and competencies as an educator that I now know I cannot do without! To pass it along to students is often the best part of our school day."

June D.,
First-Grade Teacher

"I wish I had been taught that a, i, o, and u have three sounds..."

Kris G.,
First Grade Teacher

PARENTS

"My cup runneth over. Progress is a beautiful thing. So grateful for this program."
Kelsey A.

"I learned about Raising Robust Readers through volunteering at GiGi's Playhouse New Orleans with the one-on-one Literacy Tutoring program. I was amazed by the program because I always thought that the written English language and its spelling had no rhyme or reason compared to other languages I've learned to read. The program encourages a lifestyle of learning through your environment. Another delightful thing about the program is that you can tell whether children are learning even when they can't say all of their sounds; my son can make gestures for all of the alphabet letters, although there are a few sounds he does not pronounce quite yet. I highly recommend Raising Robust Readers to anyone teaching beginning readers."
Lory L.

"Last week, my daughter, who is eighteen, was at a party where they passed out pieces of paper with questions on them as a get-to-know-you game. She shocked me by reading her question without any help and proceeded to answer it on her own! She really is learning to read and comprehend. All thanks to you two and your program!"

Kathy S.

"Simple songs and hand gestures add a fun element to learning phonograms. The methods presented through Raising Robust Readers have been very effective in not only teaching my daughter to read, but have also provided special bonding moments with Maggie."

Becky C.

"The program's simple, clear, consistent, and multi-sensory presentation is building on our son's visual memory strengths. We wish we had known about this program when our son, now eighteen, was much younger; however, we learned that it is never too late to teach the phonemic awareness skills that allow our son to decode unfamiliar words; to experience the joy of reading independently for pleasure and to be a life-long learner!

Judy and Marilee have a passion and a mission to give every individual of any age and ability the opportunity to not only learn to read; but to discover the joy, opportunities, and independence reading brings to any individual throughout their lifetime."

Jane H.

FROM FACEBOOK: PHONICS FOR FOLKS WITH DOWN SYNDROME

In addition to sharing stories, pictures, and videos, this platform gives members a community in which to ask questions, give advice, and share experiences. Here is an example of conversations that occur on our Facebook page:

This podcast was so good and all about Raising Robust Readers! I have a four-year-old, Luke, who has Down syndrome, and I'm a virtual teacher/tutor who loves and uses the Science of Reading in my tutoring. Before virtual teaching, I was in the kindergarten classroom for fourteen years. Almost all the books and journal articles I have read about teaching children with Down syndrome to read talk about learners knowing 100–500 high interest words by sight before teaching phonics. As far as I understand it, it's because they often have awesome long-term memories but not great short term memories. Would love to hear your thoughts on this and also hear from parents who are using the Raising Robust Readers program to hear if they have been successful and at what age did they first start and did they know a certain number of words first. Thanks so much. https://www.brettestevens.com/podcast-1/episode/491786df/teaching-students-with-cognitive-challenges-to-read-with-judy-ohalloran

Kristy C.

Kristy—as a former teacher and reading specialist of twenty years, I heard and read the same research. I started down that road when my son Ethan was very young. We did flash cards and Ethan memorized about twenty but never noticed them in context. I've always read a lot to both my boys. Reading is their favorite.

Ethan is now five and would be starting kinder in the next school year. (I say 'would' because I homeschool). I've been using Raising Robust Readers for a year and honestly it has been life-changing. Ethan recognizes and sees phonemes everywhere. He's in a preschool once a week and he is "teaching" his typical peers all the letter sounds. He is now noticing beginning sounds. So he will say "Mom robot starts with R." Or "Mom there is a double ee. It says E." His preschool teachers just can't believe it. One of the things that drew me to RRR is that as a former reading specialist I studied Orton Gillingham and I've seen it work miracles with people with dyslexia. RRR is so much like OG and so hands-on and multi-sensory. I just don't see how memorizing sight words is better.

Emily H.

PHONICS THE R-igh-t WAY

for Children and Adults with Down Syndrome

How Parents and Professionals Can Teach
Reading On the Go Wherever They Go

Based on the Science of Reading

JUDY O'HALLORAN & MARILEE SENIOR

PHONICS THE R-IGH-T WAY
FOR CHILDREN AND ADULTS WITH DOWN SYNDROME

How Parents and Professionals Can Teach Reading
On the Go Wherever They Go

© 2023 Minomi Publications, Inc.

Minomi Publications, Inc.
13010-4 Sandy Key Bend
North Fort Myers, FL 33903

ISBN: 979-8-9884660-0-0 (Paperback)
ISBN: 979-8-9884660-1-7 (Ebook)

www.RaisingRobustReaders.com
www.PhonicsTheRightWay.com

CONTENTS

Part Three
TEACHING PHONICS the R-IGH-T WAY

Section One: Phonograms

Section Two: Blending and Segmenting

Section Three: Syl-la-bles

Part Four
MOVING FORWARD with PHONICS the R-IGH-T WAY

Part Five
SUPPORTING PHONICS

FOREWORD

We at GiGi's Playhouse Down Syndrome Achievement Centers have instructed thousands of individuals with Down syndrome in our 1:1 Literacy Program. We find the components of the Raising Robust Readers™ phonics program, developed by the authors of *Phonics the R-igh-t Way*, to be absolutely invaluable.

Our free 1:1 Literacy Tutoring program was designed specifically to match the learning needs of individuals with Down syndrome. We first focused on teaching whole words—through rote memorization and sight words—but our students soon grew beyond this level and needed more to become functional readers.

In an effort to expand our program, our Educational Excellence Committee set out to find the very best phonics instruction for people with Down syndrome. After extensive vetting, we recognized right away that Raising Robust Readers™ presents the same teaching principles we value such as focus on the individual, respect for the child, and high expectations, and could bring our students' reading to the next level. It provides a code to phonics that is broken down into steps, is easy to understand, and uses a multi-sensory, fun, and engaging teaching approach.

We worked closely with Marilee and Judy to weave their experience and expertise into our existing curriculum. The result was a unique and personalized program that effectively teaches reading *and* reflects GiGi's mission and values.

We have incorporated the Raising Robust Readers™ program into our 1:1 Literacy Program, and we have also added the jingles to our Language, Music, 'N' Our Peeps (LMNOP) program to introduce phonemic awareness at a very early stage.

Now, with the publication of *Phonics the R-igh-t Way*, Marilee and Judy have developed yet another avenue to give parents and professionals a proven system. This book will help those with Down syndrome, of every age, move toward independent reading. We have seen it work at GiGi's Playhouse locations across the US. Now you can see it work, too.

Shari Andress, M. Ed.
National Education Manager
GiGi's Playhouse Down Syndrome Achievement Centers
www.gigisplayhouse.org

Part One

INTRODUCING PHONICS
the R-IGH-T WAY

Dream more than others think is practical.
Expect more than others think is possible.

—Claude Bissell

INTRODUCTION

Welcome. Perhaps you opened this book because you plan to take an active role in helping your child learn to read, or maybe you are just curious about phonics. In either case, you will find valuable information ahead. Rhyming jingles, meaningful gestures, and fun phonogram hunts included in this book are just the beginning steps on the path toward independent reading, greater academic accomplishments, and future opportunities. We are so glad you are here with us!

Why We Wrote This Book

The ability to sound out unfamiliar words is crucial for all readers. But if that's the case, why does our book focus just on readers with Down syndrome? Because too few of our loved ones are given the chance to prove their potential. We must elevate low expectations. We must stop relying on pictures, guessing, and memorizing (rather than sounding out) words. We want to make real reading happen. Our loved ones deserve it.

Our purpose is twofold: to enlighten and to encourage. First, we want to provide information, both from our experience and from experts in the area of reading and developmental disabilities. Secondly, we want to encourage you by affirming your beliefs in the possibilities and potential of your children and students.

"Typical" students, including those with dyslexia and learning disabilities, enter school with the expectation that they will learn to read. But far, far, far too many school districts still begin with the belief that students with Down syndrome can only memorize sight words. However, with proper instruction and a high bar of expectation, they can prove their potential to read independently.

Christopher J. Lemons, Ph.D., is an Associate Professor of Special Education in the Graduate School of Education at Stanford University and a widely-respected researcher in the area of reading and intellectual and developmental disabilities.

In his presentation, "Supporting Literacy and Inclusion for Students with Intellectual and Developmental Disabilities," Dr. Lemons shares quotes from a number of his colleagues' work. (Lemons 2022).

Over past two decades, literacy instruction has shifted from functional/sight word reading to more comprehensive literacy that includes phonological awareness, phonics, and reading comprehension. (Alhgrim-Delzell & Rivera, 2015)

My team's research has demonstrated that the sky is the limit – we do not currently know how far these students can go…but, it is farther than many have expected…(Lemons et al., 2016)

Research has demonstrated that students with IDD benefit from systematic, direct literacy instruction. (Allor et al., 2014)

Enhanced literacy skills place students on a positive trajectory for post-secondary successes including employment, independence, leisure, and happiness in life. (Browder et al., 2009)

Lemons, Christopher J.
2022 AASE National Conference

"Over the past two decades, literacy instruction has shifted from functional/sight word reading to more comprehensive literacy that includes phonological awareness, phonics, and reading comprehension." (Alhgrim-Delzell & Rivera, 2015)

"Research has demonstrated that students with IDD benefit from systematic, direct literacy instruction." (Allor et al., 2014)

In addition to these findings, Dr. Lemons adds his own findings:

"My team's research has demonstrated that the sky is the limit – we do not currently know how far these students can go...but, it is farther than many have expected...(Lemons et al., 2016). He adds, *"This population of learners can do amazing things."*

And that is why we wrote the book.

Our families and teachers, nationally and internationally, use our home or classroom Raising Robust Readers™ program, but not everyone can commit to teaching an entire phonics program. So we wrote this book—not as a reading curriculum, but to introduce a broader range of parents and professionals to what is possible.

Each of you has your own reasons for reading this book. It may be to satisfy your curiosity or raise your expectations, help you gather facts to advocate at IEPs (Individualized Education Programs), or encourage you to take an active role in expanding your child's ability to read. You may be looking for phonics strategies beyond whole word instruction for your students. Whatever your reason, we are here to help.

The Backstory

From Judy: In addition to my degree in secondary education and my experience as a classroom teacher and private tutor, I am also the mother three sons, Sean, Ryan, and Casey, our adult son who has Down syndrome. Casey is actually the genesis of this book, and also our reading program, Raising Robust Readers™.

When Casey entered public school, he was well prepared. Our family worked tirelessly to support him. He had been in an early intervention program, traveled across the state once a month for private tutoring, and attended private preschool and first grade.

But halfway through first grade, it became apparent that he would need more services. At the time, the school-district policy was to send students with Down syndrome to a segregated school. That was not acceptable to us. Casey had always been involved in typical settings and activities. Our long term goal for him was that he would, as an adult, live in his own condo, and work at a productive job in an unsegregated environment. Therefore he needed to be educated in his neighborhood school in general education classrooms. We felt sure that classrooms with their full range of *"typical"* students would prepare him for almost anything in the adult world!

So, off I went to our neighborhood school to enroll Casey for second semester. When I told Sharon Benner, the principal, that we wanted Casey fully included, she responded, "We've never done that before."

"I know," I replied. "Isn't it exciting to be starting out with a clean canvas?"

With Sharon's help in choosing the best teachers for Casey (and our unending help at home), Casey did very well until second grade, when it became clear that he would need resource help. The gap continued to widen and, with each passing year, I became more concerned, especially regarding Casey's lack of reading progress.

Since the solution was not coming from the district, I decided to start looking for the answer on my own. I researched the topic (an agonizing process before the internet), enrolled in two different universities to take fundamental reading courses, and participated in myriad teacher workshops on reading. But nothing I learned, in addition to the changing programs at school, turned Casey into an effective reader.

Then one day, I met Mary Ann Lehmann, a learning disabilities teacher who had retired from our local Catholic school. By now, Casey was a senior in high school and I had spent almost a decade looking for a method that would help him. I was in tears as I expressed my feelings of hopelessness. I would have to accept the fact that Casey would graduate being functionally illiterate.

Mary Ann tried to soothe me, then interrupted my despair to matter-of-factly interject, "He just needs an Orton-Gillingham program."

Orton-Gillingham? What's that?! And why hadn't I heard that term in reading workshops and university courses?

She went on to explain that there are things called phonograms (single letters and multi-letter combinations that show sounds) and that there is a "code," of sorts, that makes English more logical and decoding much easier. Her detailed description—unlike a lot of reading advice I had encountered—actually made sense!

Casey's father and I immediately requested an Individualized Education Program (IEP) meeting with Casey's teachers and the district transition specialist. The purposes were 1) document Casey's current reading level; 2) establish the need for an alternate reading program; and 3) have the district pay Mary Ann to implement the new program (I'll leave those details for a separate book on the importance of advocacy and knowing IDEA)—but for now, suffice it to say Mary Ann was hired by the county to come to the high school during Casey's reading period each day to tutor him. This one woman provided what the district had failed to provide: a method that explained written words and empowered Casey, in an incredibly short period, to make the quantum leap to become an effective reader!

Persistence and resolve paid off. After graduation, Casey was hired as a clerical assistant at the Lee County Courthouse. His first assignment was in the mailroom, sorting mail (good thing he could read!). He then went on to work in five departments over a twenty-year period. Casey was twice appointed by President George W. Bush to serve on the President's Committee for People with Intellectual Disabilities alongside doctors, researchers, educators, government appointees and parents. He was one of two appointees with an intellectual disability among the twenty-one professional and government members. Today, Casey lives with his wife, Megan, in a downtown apartment; uses apps to take public transportation and Ubers; monitors his bank account online; and is adept at all aspects of Amazon. He is known as the "Card Man" in the family due to his uncanny ability to pick the perfect card for each person for every holiday.

Please know that I am by no means suggesting that every individual with Down syndrome must read in order to live a fulfilling life. I do know, however, that every aspect of Casey's life has been enhanced by this ability. And my experience over many years as a very involved parent in Down syndrome communities is that whenever parents find a solution to a problem, they feel they must share it. And so I am excited to share this book with you.

From Marilee: Judy and I have been friends since before Casey was born. He calls me Mom Two.

As a child, I struggled with reading. I performed well in school but spent hours upon hours memorizing words and text to "appear" proficient when reading aloud in class. I have dyslexia. I know the struggle, and I know the shame.

When Judy began to teach her three-year-old granddaughter using the Orton-Gillingham method, I asked her if she would teach it to me so I could teach it to my granddaughters. I wanted to make sure my granddaughters would never go through what I did while learning to read. So, Judy taught me the "code" to reading.

As I learned about phonograms, I had many jaw-dropping moments. Why hadn't anyone ever told me that "igh says /i/" or "dge says /j/?" Why hadn't my teachers taken the time to explain to me that the letter "c" says /s/ when it is before e, i, and y? Finally, logic, order, and a structure that made perfect sense replaced the crazy irregular language that was so hard for me to learn as a child. I was so excited that I devoured everything I could about reading. My eyes often filled with tears as I realized that all the struggles I went through learning to read and spell never had to happen—nor should they have happened.

Judy's approach brought life to what I felt was otherwise a rather dry process. That was fine for me, but as a creative artist, I wanted our three-year-old granddaughters to have a positive introduction to reading that would be fun-filled and easy to learn. We wanted things like vowel digraphs, trigraphs, and syllables to get into, not over, the girls' heads.

We changed the academic terminology, created songs, and taught reading as we played and interacted throughout the day. We sang songs with them about Vowel Buddies and Consonant Partners, the Six Silly Syllables, and "How to Cut the Cake." Instead of rules, we talked about clues and certain misbehaving words.

I was filled with joy the day my granddaughter, Summer, then seven, hugged me and said, "Not everyone in my class likes to read because reading is so hard. But I love to read. You made it easy because you taught me the phonograms and how to cut the cake."

The concepts stuck in their heads. Instead of learning just *what* a word says, they understood *why*. In our once-a-week get-togethers over several years, they learned to read. They loved learning, and we loved teaching.

And now, we would love the opportunity to teach you phonics the right way. It has been life-changing for me. It can be life-changing for you.

The Science of Reading

There is currently a strong movement to shift away from ineffective teaching strategies such as three-cueing and whole-language methods of instruction. In the three-cueing method, students are told to 1) look at the pictures; 2) look at the first letter of the word and guess what it is; and 3) read the surrounding words and guess the word using the context. Whole-language instruction relies on the children's memorizing whole words while being exposed to "rich" literature. With systematic phonics, the reader learns letter-sound relationships through direct, explicit teaching in a clear sequence. Thus they are able to read unfamiliar words without guessing or memorizing.

On the Science of Reading website, Louisa Moats, Ed.D., a nationally recognized authority on how children learn, explains,

> The body of work referred to as the "science of reading" is not an ideology, a philosophy, a political agenda, a one-size-fits-all approach, a program of instruction, nor a specific component of instruction. It is the emerging consensus from many related disciplines, based on literally thousands of studies, supported by hundreds

of millions of research dollars, conducted across the world in many languages. These studies have revealed a great deal about how we learn to read, what goes wrong when students don't learn, and what kind of instruction is most likely to work the best for the most students.

Cindy Jiban, PhD, is the principal academic lead at Northwest Educational Assessment (NWEA), a nonprofit organization that has assessed over 4.5 million students. Dr. Jiban puts it succinctly when she explains,

> Research is clear about what matters to teach in early literacy instruction: phonological awareness, phonics and word recognition, fluency, vocabulary and oral language comprehension, and text comprehension. For each of these, a convergence of evidence tells us what works, in practice.

Unfortunately, formal research and scientific findings far too often fail to reach the end-user. Teachers wind up teaching what is dictated by the curriculum chosen by the district. Parents usually follow suit, trusting that the teachers know best.

It is our hope, then, that we can impart this critical information in a user-friendly manner to our readers. In particular, we will share with you how a more individualized approach, with a unique sequence, will support individuals with Down syndrome, their families, and teachers. And in the process of sharing this information, we hope that our deserving children with Down syndrome and other intellectual and developmental disabilities are included in the "Science of Reading" shift to more effective reading strategies. Let's give them the opportunity to prove they are "more alike than different."

Personality Perfect

In developing our method, we considered the typical characteristics of those with Down syndrome and made our method simple, clear, and consistent to complement our learners. Instructions can be easily adjusted and adapted for all ages and ability levels. Thus, when using developmentally appropriate strategies, everyone may benefit—from babies to adults and from strong readers to struggling readers.

Wait—babies?! Well, of course, we don't expect babies to be reading, but they certainly benefit when parents and caregivers sing fun songs with rhyming lyrics—and meaningful messages.

In his Mini Parenting Master Class on how music affects your brain, Dr. Ibrahim Baltagi, music education consultant and researcher, states, "Music ignites all areas of child development and skills for school readiness, particularly in the areas of language acquisition and reading skills." ("How Music Affects Your Baby's Brain: Mini Parenting Master Class," n.d.)

Babies and children, with few exceptions, love music. Let's take advantage of that early on. For instance, with babies and very young children, we can move their arms and legs to do gestures that accompany phonogram jingles. As they get older, toddlers can do the gestures by themselves as you sing songs. We explain more in Chapter 8, How to Teach a Phonogram.

What Sets Us Apart

Raising Robust Readers™ incorporates the best practices reported by highly recognized national reading organizations such as the National Reading Panel, the National Right to Read Foundation and the National Center for Learning Disabilities. It reflects the principles of the Science of Reading. Thus, multi-sensory, explicit, and systematic instruction of phonics is at the core of our program. But, even more important are the "real-life" best practices, the ones that can only come from experience, from trial and error, from learning what works best. *From parenting and teaching and living Down syndrome.*

This added dimension became the driving force for developing an approach that diverges from typical conventional phonics instruction. In the section on "Confusion Within Traditional Phonics: in Chapter 2, we explain why we do not:

- Teach single letter/single sound decoding.
    - In this approach, a word such as *neighbor* would be sounded out one letter at a time: n-e-i-g-h-b-o-r-h-o-o-d resulting in a mumbled string of letters not the word.

- "Resort" to sight words;
    - When you can't sound out a word such as r-e-a-d, letter by letter, you "resort" to making it a sight word.

- Drill word families;
    - Word families are combinations like *at, in, est,* that appear frequently as a unit in words. But they still have separate sounds.

- Begin with consonant–*short vowel*–consonant (C-V-C) blending.
    - When we drill this pattern, such as dog, cat, map, etc., using the short vowel sound, then our children think the vowel sounds are short every time.

Our unique sequence of instruction (Chapter 3—English is Not a Crazy Language) was developed from our firsthand knowledge of Down syndrome and is presented in a child-centered, multi-sensory manner. It gives learners the necessary clarity, consistency, and confidence to keep progressing. Each phase is designed to be worked through in small, successful steps from simple to complex, from sounds to syllables, and beyond to practical applications in real life.

Using this Book

We suggest reading through all the chapters first so our method can speak to your purpose in reading: curiosity, advocacy, or instruction. The most important thing is to clearly understand how your hopes and expectations can become a reality.

This book is a practical overview of how you can include reading strategies on the go, wherever you go, throughout your busy day from the classroom to the playground or the car to the pantry. We don't want you to feel like you are reading a textbook, so we purposely minimized citations within the text. You can find references and resources in the Afterword.

If you are a more casual reader—rather than a reader who plans on teaching your child or students—it is perfectly fine to focus on Part One and just skim through Part Two, which is much more detailed. Part Two is designed for those readers who need sufficient information and examples to start teaching phonics the r-igh-t way or to simply have a deeper understanding.

Note: We refer to names and sounds of letters throughout the book. When you see letters within slash marks //, you pronounce the sounds, /k/ /a/ /t/, not the names, of the letters. The terms "letters" and "phonograms" are used interchangeably throughout the book.

Discover the Path, Then Make It New

We believe this adage, "Discover the path, then make it new," really sums up our journey. We discovered the path to phonics through phonograms when Casey was in high school, but we knew we could redesign the presentation of this path in a way that would make it more engaging and effective.

Deep in our hearts, we felt an obligation—a calling, if you will—to share this new path with those of you who hope and dream that your child will become a functional, independent reader.

We invite you to join us by using this book to explore this new path in your classroom. And for those parents who choose to lead your child down this path toward more independence and opportunities, we have a message: you already have the skills. We promise you that! We are just here to help you discover them.

Blessings,
Judy and Marilee

Note from Judy and Marilee: for simplicity, we use a plural pronoun with both singular and plural antecedents. (Your child can demonstrate their skills.) Also, rather than repeatedly saying "children or students," going forward we will simply use "child" or "children" to refer to those who will be taught the lessons in this book. Teachers should not have a problem substituting "student" for "child." As for parents, our children are always our children, regardless of age.

Part Two

UNDERSTANDING PHONICS the R-IGH-T WAY

Part One introduces you to the concepts and principles of phonogram-specific phonics.

Whether you plan to take an active role in teaching your child to read or not, this part of the book will give you an understanding of why and how children need to have a strong foundation in reading phonetically. It will help you recognize—and advocate for—your child's potential to go beyond the ABCs and sight words.

CHAPTER 1

SIGHT WORDS and SOUND WORDS

From Judy: When Casey was two, I attended a workshop on Down syndrome and reading. It was all about sight words and flashcards. When I got home, I immediately started making word cards. I had them tacked all over the house and taped to objects inside and out. Casey did well learning the words. I was just tickled when he would set out "name cards" at dinner time and equally delighted by his sense of confidence and pride.

But there came a time that I, like many parents, realized that, in the long run, there are significant limitations to this focus.

Let's take a look at when memorizing whole words through approaches like flashcards may be beneficial...and when it is not.

WHEN SIGHT WORDS ARE USEFUL

1. A Sense of Hope

When our children rattle off memorized words, it gives us hope that they will become readers. It confirms our dreams and answers our prayers. We take it as a sure sign that they can read words now and will read books in the future. That is a feel-good reason, and even a good, motivating beginning for the journey...for us and them.

2. A Visual Bridge

Whole words are a bridge between oral language and print. When we attach word cards to objects around the house, we show a relationship between objects and print. There is a purpose to those "squiggly lines." These labels show the names of items. They tell us about the concrete objects to which they are attached: chair, wall, light, dress, truck, red. For older children, this connection becomes even more meaningful as they enter more formal reading instruction. Those word cards now provide "prior knowledge" and bring forth meaning when they read a sentence and see these familiar words in print on a page. (Mom sits in the chair.)

Non-readers learn that the people who read to them aren't just making up stories to go along with pictures in a book. They are actually making sense of that print on the page. That print gives us messages, and that is a vital concept to grasp.

3. Meaningful Words

Meaningful words, such as family names, can be used to create "Personal Books." The association between picture and print progresses when taken off word cards and put into book form. Further, individualized, personal stories and pictures raise a child's level of interest and memory.

I see Mom.
I see Dad.
I see my sister Jane.

4. High-Frequency Words

You can extend "decodable" sentences for interest and comprehension activities. When we include some high-frequency words (typically connecting words and prepositions such as *and, but, so, in, at*), we create longer, more complex, and interesting sentences.

> *Early Decodable:* I see a bee.
> *Longer with high-frequency words:* I see a bee in the tree.

> *Early Decodable:* I see Jay. I see Kay.
> *Longer with high-frequency words:* I see Jay and Kay at the bay.

These words can be presented as high-frequency words in an effort to allow children to read longer sentences more independently. As a transition, shared reading is effective when adults read the high-frequency words, and children read the decodable words. For example, the adult would read the high frequency words, and the child reads the decodable words (in bold) in the following sentence: **I** see **Jay**, **Kay**, and **Ray** at the **bay**.

5. "Misbehaving" Words

"Misbehaving words" just don't play by the rules, but the good news is that there are just a few for beginning readers. Some of these words like *have* and *give*, actually play by the rules. That's because English words do not end in "v," so we add a silent e. But, at an early stage, it just makes sense to memorize a few words such as:

was, were,
do, does, doing
said, says,

have, give

you, your, yours

where, what, why, who

once, one, come, some, done, none

to, too, two

very, many, laugh

WHEN SIGHT WORDS ARE NOT USEFUL

1. Low Expectations

Some students are never given the chance to move beyond sight words. Some are introduced to phonics, but "fail." That is a sure sign, some will advise, that sight words are the only answer. However, in many cases, it is not the child that fails. It is the type of instruction that fails. Entire school-district reading policies may be set up on the premise that children with Down syndrome cannot learn phonics. But this book will prove otherwise.

2. The «Cop Out»

You can't sound out *"eight"* letter by letter. It will make no sense. So what is the traditional alternative? Make it a sight word. But there is a better alternative! Teach children that *e-i-g-h* says the "long a" sound /ā/. Then they don't have to memorize *weight, eighteen, freight, eighty,* or *neighborhood.* (See the Appendices D, E, and F for charts of sounds and symbols.)

3. When Ignoring Scientific Data

Scientific studies show that the human brain is wired to "sound out" words, not memorize them. Dr. Stanislas Dehaene, neuropsychologist and professor at College de France and author of Reading in the Brain: The Science and Evolution of a Cultural Invention, explains that just exposing learners to whole words will not have them absorb the reading system. He goes on to state, "We know the right way is the explicit teaching of correspondence between letters and sounds..."

Stanford Graduate School of Education Professor Dr. Bruce McCandliss, through a series of tests using EEGs and brain mapping, found that "beginning readers who focus on letter-sound relationships, or phonics, increase activity in the area of their brains best wired for reading." (Wong 2015)

4. Limited Storage

One school district website asserts that a fourth-grader should know 1,000 sight words. Surely, storing forty-four sounds and seventy-two phonograms is easier than keeping 1,000 words in memory.

There are only so many words we can memorize. It is highly improbable, more likely impossible, that your child could memorize enough words to correctly read the texts in math, science, and geography classes. Or the labels on packages. Or the directions on a new video game. Or, eventually, a job application.

5. When Ignoring Phonological Awareness

The awareness of sounds in language, and the ability to manipulate them, is cited repeatedly as one of the greatest predictors of reading success. Memorizing whole words does not include instruction and practice in phonemic awareness. Since auditory and speech learning typically lag behind visual learning for our children, making sure they have ample and early practice is important. Spending time practicing sounds rather than sight words is much more beneficial in the long run, not only for reading but for speech and articulation.

SOUND WORDS

We want to acknowledge early on two factors that will affect how sounds will be pronounced. First, are regional accents. The "a" in Boston is not going to sound like the "a" in Baton Rouge. The second factor is the speech articulation challenges our children typically display. We can't expect perfection. We model the best sounds we can produce, and accept the best sounds our children can provide.

Teaching to a child's strengths, such as vision, is an important practice. But we should not do so to the disservice of the skills that are delayed. It should be all the more reason to begin early and practice auditory skills more frequently. Not only will receptive and expressive language skills on their own be strengthened, but the effect on reading will be enhanced.

Playing games that emphasize sounds early on will give children a good head start for phonetic reading. "What rhymes with cat? pig or hat?" "What rhymes with house? mouse, or bed?" Raffi's *Down by the Bay* is great fun and allows you to add your own crazy rhymes. Your child can respond orally or with signs.

Associating sounds with individual letters and multi-letter phonograms is also good practice. Play a memory game with phonogram cards. Have your child say (or sign) the sound as they turn each card right side up.

Make Bingo cards with phonograms that have been taught. The "caller" says a sound, and the child puts a marker on the correct printed letter.

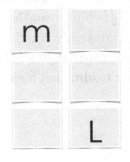

Often, parents and teachers have commented on how much clearer their children speak and how much easier it is to understand them after they have started learning individual phonogram sounds. It is our experience that if classroom teachers and speech pathologists collaborate, progress is often accelerated in both areas.

In the next chapter, we will explain why "traditional" phonics can be confusing and frustrating, especially for our individuals with Down syndrome. This is understandably one of the reasons parents and professionals fall back on sight words. They want what is best for their children. So let's look at how we can provide a proven approach to teaching phonics.

But before doing so, we offer a list of definitions associated with phonics. While we strive to use more user-friendly words than scholarly ones, these are important terms that we do include in this book. They are used more in academic circles than in casual conversations, but they are important to know. We provide them here before moving on to why conventional phonics may not work.

USEFUL DEFINITIONS
(Appendix A)

SPOKEN LANGUAGE TERMS
Phon—hear   ology—the study of

PHONICS is a method of teaching people to read based on the sounds that letters represent.

PHONEMES are the smallest parts of sound in spoken words. For instance, there are three sounds in the spoken word cat /k/ /ă/ /t/. There are also three sounds in the spoken word caught /k/ /aw/ /t/, even though that word has six letters. Generally, we recognize forty-four sounds in the English language. Please note that when you see letters within slash marks //, you pronounce the sound, not the name, of the letter.

PHONEMIC AWARENESS is the ability to identify and manipulate individual sounds in spoken words. "Bat" begins with the initial sound /b/. "Tab" ends with the final sound /b/. Being able to move sounds and decode the words indicates skill in phonemic awareness.

PHONOLOGICAL AWARENESS is a broader term that includes phonemic awareness. It, too, refers to spoken words, but it also includes identifying and manipulating larger parts of spoken language, such as syllables and sentences.

WRITTEN LANGUAGE TERMS
gram; graph—written

LETTERS, in general, refer to the twenty-six symbols that make up the English language. They can also combine to create multi-letter phonograms, such as "ay" or "eigh."

PHONOGRAMS are single letters (the alphabet) and two (oa)-, three (igh)-, and four-letter (eigh) combinations that show just one sound. For instance, the single-letter phonogram "f" represents the sound /f/, and the two-letter phonogram "ph" also represents the sound /f/. Generally recognized, there are seventy-two basic phonograms in English. (Appendix B)

GRAPHEMES are written symbols that represent a sound (phoneme). This can be a single letter or a combination of letters, as noted above. When we say the sound /p/, this is a phoneme; but when we write the letter "p," it is a grapheme.

ORTHOGRAPHIC refers to that part of language that involves letters and spelling.

TAKEAWAY

The overall message is that there comes a time for moving beyond meaningful sight word memorization. In order to be independent readers who are able to read unfamiliar text as well as familiar words, children must move beyond the ABCs and sight words. Visual skills are a strength for individuals with Ds. Using that strength to memorize individual phonograms rather than simply sight words will lead to more independent reading.

MY NOTES

CHAPTER 2

A *SOUND* APPROACH to READING
But Why Conventional Phonics May Fail

The phrase, A "Sound" Approach, carries a double meaning. The first has to do with **hearing**, and the second has to do with being **effective**.

A SOUND *HEARING* APPROACH

When we approach reading through phonics, we are teaching reading based on phonemes or sounds represented by single- and multi-letter phonograms.

It is a sound-word approach, not a sight-word approach—meaning, it connects printed words to *spoken* language by putting the sounds in those words together. It gives instruction and practice to phonemic awareness, one of the strongest predictors of proficient reading.

MRI scans now show brain activity during reading. This gives positive, scientific information that allows neuroscientists to see how the brain works during whole word reading and letter/sound reading.

Dr. Dehaene has coined the term "letterbox." This term describes the proximity of three areas of the brain: 1) visual (especially letter recognition), 2) word meaning, and 3) word pronunciation and articulation. Thus, these brain circuits connect spoken language and printed words in the brain, leading Dr. Dehaene to explain, "We know the right way is the explicit teaching of correspondences between letters and sounds."

Language and Reading

Speaking a language, with a few exceptions, comes naturally to humans. Children absorb what they hear and they instinctively repeat what they hear—or, at least, they try to mimic the words we give them. Reading, on the other hand, does *not* come naturally. Children do not learn to read by simply hearing someone else read. It must be taught. They must learn the print/sound correlation. Evolution has hard-wired the brain for language...any language. But evolution has not hard-wired the brain for reading. Steven Pinker, a cognitive scientist at Harvard University, puts it rather poetically: *"Children are wired for sound, but print is an optional accessory that must be painstakingly bolted on."*

Oral language is actually the first step in reading. Talking to our children, singing to them, and reading (especially reading rhyming books) enable them to hear and process language. It builds vocabulary. The more words children are exposed to and grow to understand, the better their vocabulary and comprehension. Our children with receptive and expressive challenges especially benefit from intervention and practice in this area. We may need to speak a little slower, but we definitely need to speak...and speak frequently.

Again, since auditory skills are not typically a strong suit for our children, it makes sense to begin working on this skill early and practice it often. Describe things you do, you see, and even what you are thinking. This will stimulate their nerve pathways. But if you have concerns, you should seek professional evaluation.

Clare Cronin—AuD, CCC-A, and Doctor of Audiology—advises:

> ...contacting an audiologist for monitoring of hearing is advisable. If your child is young, a pediatric audiologist, especially those at children's hospitals, will have the most knowledge about and experience with children who have Down syndrome. Parents are generally aware that schools have Speech and Language Pathologists on faculty. But some schools also employ Educational Audiologists who can ensure that hearing needs unique to schools and classrooms are met if a longer-term hearing problem is found.

Speech/Language Impairment

Parents of children who are non-verbal may think their children can't read because they cannot articulate the sounds correctly—but think about it. You are reading this book silently, as you most likely do the majority of your reading. The reality is that your child can read, and you can incorporate methods to accommodate them.

Your child can demonstrate their reading and comprehension skills in various ways. Children do not have to say /j/ to prove they know the sound of "j." To build this association, you can pronounce the /j/ sound and have your child give you the "j" card from a group of letter cards. Or, they can circle the correct picture (a pink pig, a white sheep, a gray sheep, etc.) after they read the sentence, "See the gray sheep." Or, they can choose the green boat (not the green truck or the blue boat) after they read the sentence, "Pick up the green boat." Reading and comprehension can be clearly demonstrated, without speaking a word!

Deaf and Hard of Hearing

Parents of individuals who are deaf or hard of hearing may disregard phonics, thinking their children cannot learn to read phonetically since they cannot hear sounds correctly. Teach the jingles and individual sounds by using American Sign Language. Sounds such as /oy/, /aw/, and /ch/ may not have a sign. In that case, you can simply make up your own gesture. Just be sure it makes sense, and be consistent when using it. Your child can sign the words when reading controlled vocabulary readers that you create. If you create any unique signs, be sure to share them with others who help your child with reading.

Rachel Sieg, MA, CCC, SLP, Speech-Language Pathologist, works with a ten-year-old boy who has been hard of hearing since he was six. She notes excitedly, "His speech improved when he began reading. "He could see the words on paper, not just see the signs for the words."

A SOUND *EFFECTIVE* APPROACH

The Nation's Report Card

You can find details of reading scores reported by the National Assessment of Educational Progress (NAEP) at www.nationsreport-card.gov. It states, "In 2022, the average reading score at both fourth and eighth grade decreased by three points compared to 2019."

That's perfectly understandable, given Covid and virtual schooling took place in 2020. However, even in 2019, approximately two-thirds of fourth and eighth graders in the United States were already reading *below* proficiency. It is shocking to learn that almost 66 percent of America's fourth- and eighth-grade students could not read proficiently—that is, were not mastering age and grade-level expectations.

We Wondered: What Went Wrong?

While there are many reasons that can affect learning, research-based studies over years already showed that non-phonics-based methods, such as the popular three-cueing and whole language methods, commonly used in schools, are ineffective. Our common sense and personal experiences told us the same thing. So, to help us understand what could be going wrong, we focused on phonics. It appeared to us that the "traditional" phonics approach could confuse, frustrate, and even fail children who are not what we call "natural" readers. "Natural" readers seem to be able to learn how to read regardless of what you put in front of them or what approach you take. They practically teach themselves!

We wanted to develop a program that was phonics-based, easy for parents to teach, and effective for individuals with Down syndrome and others with cognitive challenges.

Let's take a look at the not-so-great traditional phonics methods we analyzed. While you are reading, think of your own child, and imagine the effect these might have on them.

CONFUSION WITHIN TRADITIONAL PHONICS

One Sound/One Letter Phonics

In this type of phonics, students are taught to look at a letter and say its sound, then go to the next letter and say its sound, and so on. However, you can't sound out the word e-i-g-h-t and come up with "eight." How do you explain how to read "eight" to a beginning reader when the letter "a" isn't even in the word? You can't! So, you resort to teaching hundreds and hundreds of "sight" words and tons of exceptionalities.

Word Families

Countless phonics programs teach word families. The theory makes sense: take a shortcut and build on fluency. The problem is that each letter in word families still represents a separate sound. Take the "at" family: /ă/ + /t/. After drilling and drilling and drilling, it is most likely your children will dutifully repeat the word family sound every time they see it. That works very well in a sentence like this:

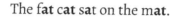

The **fat cat** sat on the **mat**.

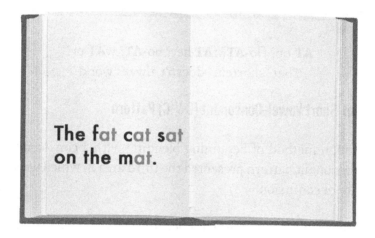

The fat cat sat on the mat.

But along comes a sentence like this...

The fat cat sat on the mat atop the float with his father in the boat on the water.

You likely read that sentence the way a proficient reader would. Now go back, and put yourself in the seat of an individual who is just learning to put sounds together to make words; who typically, by nature, likes routine, structure, and predictability; who has been drilled and drilled on the "at" family. As you come to each word with the "at," be sure to pronounce **at**, and here's what you'll get:

The **fat cat** sat on the **mat atop** the **float** with his **father** in the boat on the **water**.

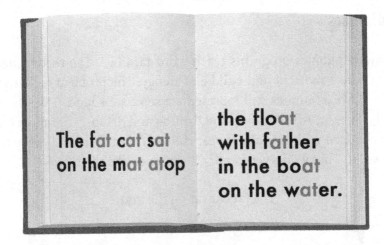

The fat cat sat on the mat atop the float with father in the boat on the water.

AT-op? flo-**AT**? f**AT**-her? bo-**AT**? w**AT**-er?
That "shortcut" doesn't always work!

Consonant–Short Vowel–Consonant (C-V-C) Pattern

The common method of beginning blending with a consonant–short vowel–consonant pattern presented the third area in which we saw the possibility of confusion.

This pattern (s-i-t, p-e-t, c-u-p) has become the standard way to introduce blending. The instruction and copious practice sheets ingrain the pattern and the short vowel sound. After all, it typically takes our learners many more repetitions than the average child. Below are six words. Try it out yourself as if you were a struggling reader. Follow the three-letter pattern with a short vowel between the consonants—sounding out each letter—and listen to the results. Remember, put yourself in the seat of a beginning reader with Down syndrome and say /ă/ in the middle of each word.

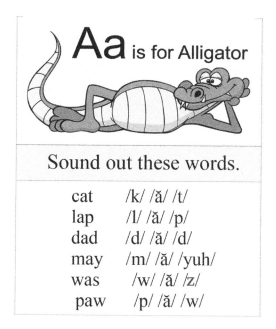

Aa is for Alligator

Sound out these words.

cat   /k/ /ă/ /t/
lap   /l/ /ă/ /p/
dad   /d/ /ă/ /d/
may   /m/ /ă/ /yuh/
was   /w/ /ă/ /z/
paw   /p/ /ă/ /w/

Did you read it the way a struggling reader would, given all the instruction and drilling with the C-V-C pattern words?

When we teach one sound (the short sound) of a vowel and drill and drill and drill this pattern, and then it doesn't work, our readers will experience confusion and frustration—and, most likely, failure. Is it any wonder that many teachers fall back on sight words and survival words and say that phonics does not work for our children?

This analysis led us to develop a studied departure from the above. In the next section, we will go into more detail on this shift.

TAKEAWAY

Two-thirds of American fourth graders and up read below proficiency. Oral language comes naturally (for most people), but reading does not. MRI scans in the area of the brain referred to as the "letterbox" can now reveal the most effective way to teach reading. To connect the visual, sounds, and meaning areas, instruction in letter/sound correspondence, that is, explicit, systematic phonics, proves the most effective. But not all phonics instruction is equal. "Conventional" phonics, in fact, has components that can confuse, frustrate, and even fail children, especially those with Down syndrome. These include: one letter/one sound correspondence; word families; and starting with C-V-C blending.

MY NOTES

CHAPTER 3

ENGLISH IS NOT A CRAZY LANGUAGE

THERE IS A CODE

There is a code for reading English that unravels the mystery of why words sound the way they do. This code has been validated by research-based studies. It has been put forth by the National Reading Panel. It has been proven by practitioners and promoted by The Science of Reading. This code shows that English is *not* a crazy language. In fact, it is logical, reliable, and predictable. The reality is that if you can read this paragraph, you already know much of the code—you just don't realize it. This book will crack that code for you and allow you to share your new knowledge in a clear and fun-filled manner.

FIVE CLUES TO CRACK THE CODE

1. Don't Stop at Z.

Look at the letters below. What's Missing?

a b c d e f g h j k l m n o p q r s t u v w x y z

Yes. The letter "i" is missing. Have you ever seen an alphabet book without the letter "i"? Of course not...unless your cherub has ripped out that page. Yet alphabet books ignore "igh." Why? After all, they make the same sound!

The alphabet, as we know it, has twenty-six letters. However, there are approximately forty-six more common letter combinations that complete this code. Phonogram "igh" is one of them.

Below is a chart that we use in our reading program (Appendix B). It goes beyond the single-letter alphabet and shows additional combinations that make up the words we read. The subscript numbers indicate how many different sounds those phonograms can represent. For instance, "Hit like a champion. Listen to me. I makes three sounds: /ĭ/ /ī/ /ē/."

The 72 Phonograms
Phonograms Show the Smallest Sounds We Read.

Alphabet Phonograms

a_3 b c_2 d e_2 f g_2 h i_3 j k l m
n o_3 p qu r s_2 t u_3 v w x_2 y_4 z

Vowel Buddy Phonograms

ai ay eigh ee igh oa oe
er ur ir ear ar_3 or_2 au aw augh oi oy
ea_3 ei_2 ey_2 ie_2 ew_2 ue_2 ui_2 ow_2 oo_3 ou_4 $ough_6$

Consonant Partner Phonograms

tch sh wh ng ph ck gn kn wr mb dge
th_2 ch_3 ed_3 ci ti si_2

© 2020 Raising Robust Readers

2. We Read by Sounds, Not by Letters

Phonics is a broad term that can mean different things to different people. But, it has typically translated to sounding out (decoding) words one letter at a time. Try to sound out *caught* one letter at a time, and you will see why many think our children cannot learn to read phonetically. This one-to-one, letter-to-sound approach is not effective for anyone, but an Orton-Gillingham, Science of Reading-based method for sounding out words *does* give reliable results.

Previously, we defined a phonogram simply as "single letters and two-, three-, and four- letter combinations that show the smallest sounds in words." As you read further, you will see that we do not take a textbook-style linguistic approach to our definitions and explanations. Instead, we make it easy enough, through jingles and verses, for even a preschooler to understand. We so enjoy the videos that parents post of their children singing and gesturing phonogram songs on our Facebook page "Phonics for Folks with Down Syndrome." In addition, time after time, parents tell us their children can still sing the jingles years later. They usually add, "I can too!"

In this example, we further define a phonogram to the tune of "Mary Had a Little Lamb." Try it below—begin by humming the familiar tune, then add the words.

<blockquote>
Phonograms are all around,
all around, all around.
Phonograms are all around
in all the words we see.

Phonograms show the smallest sounds,
smallest sounds, smallest sounds.
Phonograms show the smallest sounds
in all the words we read.
</blockquote>

A phonogram can have one letter,
have two letters, have three letters.
A phonogram can have four letters,
but only make one sound.

Some phonograms can hop around
in different words,
and change their sound.
Phonograms make just one sound
in each word that we read.

Hear the song and see the video at this YouTube link:
https://youtu.be/ZBxdaGk9T5g

3. English is Like Math; Just with Letters

We feel confident that the addition problem above on the left is one
that you can easily solve. When you think of English, try this: English is
like math. You just add sounds together, instead of numbers, to make a
word. When you look at it this way, you will realize English is *not* crazy
and impossible to understand. Rather, English is a logical language that
has certain guidelines.

We know that many individuals with Down syndrome struggle with math concepts, but remember: the clues in this section are for *you* to see how reading, writing, and spelling English is actually very logical. When you understand the logic, and guidelines (the word formulas), you can convey that in simple, multi-sensory, fun ways individualized for your child.

4. Syllable Types Tell Vowels What Sound to Make

Syllable types give you a clear and easy way to answer your child's question: "But *why* does it say that?" You no longer have to answer in exasperation, "I don't know. English is crazy! Just memorize it!" Once you understand the syllable types, you can guide your child to the correct vowel sound. Once children know the syllable types, they can say the vowel sound without guessing. This is a real game-changer for those who are further along in their reading journey.

5. Spelling and Writing: Clues to Choose Which Sound to Use

Hear the sound and write it down. When we spell by sound, there is no need to spend hours memorizing spelling words. There is no need to write a word ten, twenty, or thirty times for homework to prepare for a spelling test. Admittedly, many times, that sound can be spelled in different ways, so focusing on how the correctly spelled word looks will help. Where the sound occurs in the word can be a clue to its spelling. Showing simple visuals will help your child to remember.

away ay	pail ai
☐ ay	ai ☐ ai ☐ a̶i̶
Clue: ay is a two-letter ā that we use at the end of English words.	**Clue:** ai is a two-letter ā that we do not use at the end of English words.

TAKEAWAY

There is a "code" that proves the English language is *not* illogical and crazy. By following five clues, we can crack this code and learn to read more easily and proficiently. They are:

1. Go beyond the twenty-six alphabet letters to learn an additional forty-six multi-letter combinations
2. Decode words sound-by-sound, not letter-by-letter
3. English is like math, only with letters. 1+3+1 = 5 and r+igh+t = right
4. There are six syllable types, and they can tell a vowel what sound to make
5. There are clues to help us spell correctly

MY NOTES

....
....
....
....
....
....
....
....
....
....
....
....

CHAPTER 4

COMPREHENSION and the SIMPLE VIEW OF READING

Before we begin our explanation for teaching the phonics code, we want to discuss comprehension. We would be among the first to say that just sounding out words does not mean you're reading. Real reading means *understanding* the words on the page, on the signs, on the billboards, on the menu, on the job application, not just being able to decode words one by one.

In our program and in this book, we present meaningful and pragmatic phonics in a unique sequence, but we also make sure that comprehension strategies are woven into every step. We will give you some examples, but before we do so, it will be helpful if you understand the widely accepted theory that reading comprehension is made up of two components: decoding and language knowledge. This theory, known as the Simple View of Reading, was initially presented by Philip B. Gough and William E. Tunmer in 1986 in the journal *Remedial and Special Education*. It was first proposed to clarify the role of decoding in reading.

The Simple View of Reading is generally represented by this simple formula:

Decoding x Language Comprehension = Reading Comprehension
D x LC = RC

The Simple View of Reading

D - *Decoding* is word recognition, the ability to sound out familiar and unfamiliar words.

LC - *Language Comprehension* refers to a person's ability to understand language, i.e., spoken words, vocabulary, and syntax (the arrangement of words in a sentence).

RC - *Reading Comprehension* is understanding what the printed text is telling you.

In very "simple" terms, if you cannot Decode (sound out) unfamiliar words, you cannot read them. Likewise, if you don't understand the meaning of the words you can decode, you will not comprehend what you are reading (LC). Independent reading comprehension (RC) is only as strong as the weaker component. Therefore, we need to focus on both.

Since our children typically have delayed speech, it is essential to provide lots of purposeful conversation. We need to enhance and enrich our children's language experience every chance we get. Even if our children are language-limited or non-verbal, hearing language and learning the meaning of words is essential. If your child is deaf or hard of hearing, teach and use signs to explain new words and situations throughout the day. And, of course, our children need many, many, many more opportunities and practice to master skills in language comprehension.

The main focus of *Phonics the R-igh-t Way* is on Decoding. We are committed to teaching strategies that enable our children to "sound out" words independently. But we know the other half of reading comprehension is language. Therefore, we bring in language strategies at all stages to build toward the overall goal: comprehension.

Below are a few examples of activities that illustrate how to teach comprehension and decoding in tandem. These will set the stage for the coming chapters in "Teaching the Code." By paying attention to how we embed comprehension from the very beginning, you can apply the same strategies throughout the book and throughout your everyday teaching.

COMPREHENSION and PHONOGRAMS

We use songs, print, gestures, and physical associations to introduce each phonogram and add activities to expand vocabulary and establish prior knowledge. For example, in Chapter 8, we suggest watching videos of stingrays ahead of teaching our sample phonogram "ay." Otherwise, how does "I see a ray in the bay" make sense when you live in Nebraska? The gesture and the prop further enhance the new words and facilitate remembering them. In this manner, we incorporate our child's visual strengths and support working memory.

COMPREHENSION and PICTURE CONVERSATION (Hear It, See It)

Let's use phonogram D as an example. The page presents the jingle and a picture of a happy worm digging up daisies on a sunny day.

Dd

The name of the letter is d.
The sound of the letter is /d/.

d says /d/.
d says /d/.
Dig up **d**aisies.
d says /d/.

Dd   **/d/**

Dig up **d**aisies.

The name of the letter is D.
The sound of the letter is /d/.

D says /d/.
D says /d/.
Dig up daisies.
D says /d/.

Before we bring attention to the name and sound of the phonogram, we talk about the picture. If your child is too young or not developmentally ready to answer questions, you will provide the information as you point to the parts of the picture. For those who are able to answer questions, some of the interactions would include:

Specific questions: *Name some things you see in this picture. What color is the sky? What color are the flowers?*

Unknown words: *These flowers are called daisies. They usually have white petals and yellow centers. There is one flower on each stem. The stem holds the leaves and the flowers. Can you say 'daisy?'*

Critical thinking questions: *Why do you think the cute worm is wearing a hat? Why is he wearing gloves? Do you have a favorite flower?*

After talking about the picture, you can begin teaching the name and sound of the phonogram and introducing the jingle. Have that conversation continue and spill over into other parts of your day. If they are in season, bring a pot of daisies to your classroom. Include *Wildflower* by Melanie Brown in your reading center. Take a family trip to a garden store and buy flowers to plant outside or enjoy inside. Go to the library and look for books about daisies.

COMPREHENSION and VOCABULARY

We designed the jingles and gestures not just to include words that contain the sound, but to extend the phonogram activity and include language experiences. For example, in the phonogram jingles for "l" and "r," children learn "Lift my left hand" and "Raise my right hand." Thus, they learn the phonogram names and sounds, and they learn directional words at the same time. This allows parents and teachers to weave language knowledge into the phonics activity and have it flow over to many other opportunities. It creates early occasions for later practical applications, such as comprehending a math worksheet that says, "Add the numbers on the right side of the page." Children will then have both components to understand the directions.

$$D \text{ (r-igh-t)} \times LC \text{ (right side)} = RC \text{ (understanding)}$$

In the "dge" phonogram jingle, we chose a common and an uncommon word to illustrate the sound and expand vocabulary. The rhyme says, "We gave her a nudge and an ice cream fudge." "Ice cream fudge" is easy to relate to. You can go to the grocery store and buy a box of fudge bars. Talk about the word fudge. Compare it to chocolate. Contrast it with vanilla. All the while, you enjoy a special time together.

"Nudge" is a little more unusual, but still easy to teach. Talk about and (gently) demonstrate the difference between a nudge and a push. When is it okay to push? (swing, stroller.) When would you nudge? (to gently get Dad's attention)

Later when your middle-schooler is reading a sentence in a short story, such as, *"Bonnie gave Jenny a nudge and told her to say thank you to Mom,"* they will have the background knowledge to make sense of the sentence. They won't have to rely on a faulty three-cueing system that will not help them comprehend what they have just read. Three-cueing wouldn't work here, because:

- There is no <u>picture</u> to help read the words.
- The word starts with "n," so they might <u>guess</u> nickel, napkin, note, nest...
- The <u>context</u> doesn't help. Bonnie could give Jenny a nacho, and it would technically make sense.

COMPREHENSION and DECODABLE READERS

We have created controlled vocabulary readers that focus on targeted multi-letter phonograms while reinforcing and building on previous ones. Since children have different areas of interest, it's not likely that the areas of interest in our Train the Brain Readers will coincide with your child's, but that's not what they were designed to do. You can create personal books that reflect your child's interests. Include words that contain the focused phonograms plus ones already studied. In that manner, you are working on both authentic word reading and comprehension through high-interest text.

At the end of our Train the Brain Readers, we include factual comprehension questions that target the typical who, what, when, where questions. But we also include discussion questions that encourage deeper thinking. "What would you like to do at the bay?" "If you could take a friend, whom would you take? Why?" Inference questions such as, "Why do you think Sallie took an umbrella when she left the house?" extend critical thinking.

Connecting reading experiences to real-life experiences is especially effective. For instance, one of our parents wrote to tell us about her daughter and the connection she made with the Train the Brain Reader, *Gus*. She explained, "Last night, we worked on the short U reader. We just laughed and laughed, because I am always telling her in the shower to 'scrub, not rub' her hair. To see Gus dealing with a similar issue was wonderful. I wish I had recorded her sounding out 'scrub,' and the look on her face when she realized she knew exactly what that word was. I don't think we will ever have trouble with the short U sound again!"

COMPREHENSION and SYLLABLES

Children who have mastered decoding (taking apart) and encoding (putting together) are ready to learn about syllables (Chapter 14). It is important to ensure our children have retained the meaning of familiar terms such as "vowels" and "consonants" and to explain the meanings of new vocabulary terms such as "open" and "closed." We progress from single-syllable to multiple-syllable words, giving us a terrific opportunity to introduce more complex expressions that expand vocabulary. For instance, the one-syllable word "school" can lead to "preschoolers" and the ability to expand and understand language.

Environmental words such as "Avenue," "grocery," "menu," "detergent," etc. are perfect for syllable division instruction and practice. In addition, it is important to use meaningful vocabulary for those older children who are given assignments in various academic subjects. Use words found in their textbooks such as "instruction," "example," "multiple choice," "practice," "government," "biology," "continent," and so on. There are so many choices for meaningful words, you don't need to struggle to think of words to divide. Just look around.

COMPREHENSION and the "23° TILT AND TEACH"

Phonics does not have to be—nor should it be—a dull, isolated, rote skill. Decoding is a skill that can come alive when teamed with Language Comprehension, especially when there is a real-world purpose.

We have a simple strategy for combining the two skills to take advantage of your environment and resources in a simple, easy, woven manner. We call it the "23° Tilt and Teach" method. Here's how it works. First, look at what you are doing—anything in your daily life—from a slightly (that's why we say 23°) different angle. Then, look at the resources you have on hand already. Look in your real-world environment. Finally, ask yourself, "How can I notice this from a different perspective and use this resource to help my child practice their reading skills?"

Examples for families:

- As you pass a Jeep in the parking lot of your grocery store, play "I Spy Double e." You can change the jingle and sing, "Double e says /ē/. Double e says /ē/. A Jeep, I see. A Jeep, I see. Double e says /ē/."

- During bath time with tub toys, sing, "O-a makes an /ō/. O-a makes an /ō/. It's fun to float on my boat. O-a makes an /ō/." Sing the jingle again, inserting the color of a boat, "It's fun to float on my red boat. O-a makes an /ō/." Then have your child choose the corresponding boat. Repeat with each differently colored boat. Now you have reviewed colors as well as sounds.

- After diapering your baby, "march" their legs and arms and say in a sing-song way, "The name of the letter is M. The sound of the letter is /m/. M says /m/. M says /m/. March to music. M says /m/." This can be done anywhere your child is on their back— the sofa, your lap, etc. Be sure to put your face close to theirs when saying that last, drawn-out "mmmmmmm" so they can see your lips, and you can see their smile and hear their giggles.

Examples for teachers:

- During calendar time in the classroom, have children find the phonogram "ay" in each day of the week. Point out the "ay" in the word "crayon," and hold up a gray crayon and a green crayon. Say each color, holding the "a" and the "e" sound. Ask the children which one says /ā/.

- For Show and Tell time, have children bring in phonogram clues/ props for the sound you are studying. Send the phonogram jingle home and tell parents ahead of time. Lots of pluses here: 1) Parents learn the jingle and can practice at home; 2) Children get excited to share; 3) if they have permission, children can add it to the "Treasure Clue Box" instead of taking it back home. Just imagine how many different Clue Box treasures you can accumulate without any expense to you!

- Children don't have to learn the ABCs in order. They can learn H at Halloween time and V in February for Valentine. At Thanksgiving, they can even find the two-letter phonogram "Th" in classroom book titles on your bookcase. The classroom is your workbook, and environmental print becomes your extra worksheets.

The point is to realize that the ordinary things you typically do, like walking through a parking lot, bath time, playing with the baby, and calendar time, can become extraordinary opportunities to expand D x LC = RC. Your day will be filled with a galaxy of opportunities to practice phonemic awareness, train the brain to "see sounds," and expand language. A slight tilt in how you look at life makes a big difference.

COMPREHENSION STRATEGIES

Comprehension strategies can begin with very young children and progress to more complex strategies, especially for older children. Read-Alouds and Think-Alouds are good to begin. You can start modeling comprehension by doing them even with very young ones. When reading aloud to your child, use your voice in an engaging manner that reflects the print (whisper, scared, growling) and ask questions to make the story come alive. For example, as you read *How Do Dinosaurs Say Good Night* by Jane Yolen and Mark Teague, act out the action words in this series of questions:

"Does he *mope*, does he *moan*, does he *sulk*, does he *sigh?*"

When we model Think-Alouds, we help children realize that there can be thoughts in their heads as they read. When they are aware of these thoughts, they can become more engaged in the book. As a result, their comprehension—and enjoyment—increases.

The following part of a conversation takes place in *The Pout-Pout Fish and the Worry-Worry Whale*, a popular rhyming book by Deborah Diesen:

"Is something wrong?" asked Mr. Fish.
"I'd like to help, if so."
"It's the party," answered Willa Whale.
"I *don't* want to go!"

Before turning the page, you could stop and reflect (slowly and aloud) with phrases like these:

- Hmmmm, I wonder what's wrong.
- I guess that's why she is called the Worry-Worry Whale.
- I wonder why Willa doesn't want to go to the party. I love to go to parties, don't you?
- I wonder what kind of party it is. Maybe it's a birthday party.
- It sure is nice of Mr. Fish to want to help. I'll bet he does. Gosh, I can't wait to find out.

As children get older, you can present more complex strategies to help with their school assignments. When employing these more complex steps, use the I do, We do, You do method (Chapter 6). You can guide your children through these steps with each new passage until they can do it independently. Even with older children, ample practice is necessary.

SQ3R is an example of a very valuable yet doable technique. When Casey was younger, he was invited on several occasions to present to university students majoring in education. In one of his presentations, he took the students through his favorite comprehension method. That was twenty-five years ago, and he still remembers the steps. Here are the guidelines he gave them for helping students go through a reading assignment:

- **S**urvey - Look over the assignment and talk about it. Discuss any unfamiliar words. Pay attention to the title, subtitles, captions, pictures, bold print, colored print, etc.
- **Q**uestion - If there are questions at the end of the assignment, read them first. Then ask yourself: "What questions do I have? What am I wondering about? What do I hope to learn?"
- **R**ead - Take one paragraph (or less) at a time. Read each twice (or more) if necessary before going on. This helps develop focus and working memory until you can read longer sections without losing concentration.
- **R**ecite - Talk (tell someone else) about what you think the main points are. What details do you remember?
- **R**eview - Go back to the text and check on what you remembered. Did you get it right? If you get it wrong, that's okay, because now you know the right answer.

As you can see, a more formal, targeted comprehension process is lengthy. A lot of complex thinking is going on during this activity. For that reason, you should not turn this into a detailed decoding lesson as well. While reading, you can offer a little assistance on sounding out challenging words, but you want to focus on the language process. You can use those challenging words in a separate decoding session.

In her 2018 article in BU Journal of Graduate Studies in Education, "Reading: Children with Down Syndrome," Mireille Bazin-Berryman concludes:

> ...word recognition, phonological awareness, orthographic knowledge, and reading comprehension must specifically be taught to all children, but in particular to children with Down syndrome in a way that is conducive to their reading and learning profile. Teacher education must include the different ways to intervene in reading

for children with Down syndrome because of the prevalence of these children in our regular stream classrooms. Successfully teaching children with Down syndrome to read provides them an effective mode of communication, which in turn supports their inclusion in society, their contribution to society, and their autonomy.

As you read forward in the coming chapters, be aware of the opportunities you have to include language in your lessons and in your everyday activities. The more practice our children have in receptive and expressive interaction, the stronger these skills will become. And the stronger these skills become, the stronger reading comprehension becomes.

TAKEAWAY

The Simple View of Reading explains that real reading is made up of two parts: decoding and language. If either is missing, comprehension will be negatively affected. Even if our children are deaf or hard of hearing, they can experience many varied language experiences through sign language. Decoding, then, need not be an isolated, dull, or rote skill. When we look at our actions and environment from a slightly different perspective (23° tilt), we can easily incorporate our activities and weave them into purposeful experiences that will support Reading Comprehension.

MY NOTES

....

....

....

....

....

....

CHAPTER 5

THE SUCCESS is in the SEQUENCE

11 STEPS TO SUCCESS

The feature that most sets our approach apart from other Orton-Gillingham-based programs is our unique sequence of teaching phonograms and syllables. When we considered the typical personality qualities of individuals with Down syndrome, we designed the journey with them in mind, using small steps that build on success. We looked at how the order of instruction could facilitate that success. Just as a travel agent who has visited a country over and over has a keen insight into the locals and "must-see" destinations, we have decades of hands-on insight into the personalities and learning styles of those with Down syndrome. We have adjusted our sequence of instruction to match.

Even for those readers who do not intend to take the lead role in teaching, it is most beneficial to understand how a new sequence can lead to new results. Here's a general description of that sequence. We go into more details in future chapters. Keep in mind that we must always focus on the individual child, not the steps. Please modify the sequence as needed to fit your child.

1. Single-Sound Consonants

b, d, f, h, j, k, l, m, n, p, qu, r, t, v, w, z

We begin here because children have been introduced to the alphabet through the alphabet songs and numerous alphabet books at home and at school. They are familiar with the letters, so we begin with familiarity. However, at this point, we only concentrate on the letters with one sound. Why? Because when there is only one choice, this eliminates confusion and leads your child to success, especially when they start to blend. Note: the consonants above are in alphabetical order. In Chapter 6, you will learn guidelines for introducing them in a more effective sequence.

2. Train the Brain with Double E

We use "Double e" to train the brain to see these two letters as a unit—as one sound. This gives us an opportunity to compare a single-letter with a double-letter phonogram. The comparison is easy to make because the *double*-letter phonogram "ee" has the same letters as the *single*-letter phonogram "e." We talk about, and demonstrate, the difference between single and double, allowing us to incorporate language comprehension. At this stage, the goal is not to read the word, but simply to spot "Double e" in words. If possible, your child can chime in with "'Double e' says *e*" when pointing to the "ee."

3. Vowel Buddies
ai, ay, eigh, ee, igh, oa, oe

All words need vowels, but instead of teaching the sounds of the alphabet vowels—those single letter vowels (a, e, i, o, u, y) all of which have *multiple* sounds—we introduce the "Vowel Buddies." This accomplishes three things:

- We continue to train the brain to "see sounds," not just see letters in words;
- We present vowel phonograms that make only one sound;
- When learning to blend, there is only one choice per phonogram—hence, success is built in.

You don't want to drill and drill and drill your beginning reader with the short vowel sound only to confuse them later with different sounds for that vowel. Doing so is only asking for a meltdown moment.

4. Introducing ay

You can add the phonogram "ay" to the end of each newly mastered Single-Sound Consonant to form additional words with just two sounds: *bay, day, Fay,* etc. Children actually enjoy the Vowel Buddy phonograms because they are a departure from what they have been introduced to and exposed to for some time. They enjoy and appreciate the novelty of going beyond the ABCs.

5. Controlled Vocabulary Readers

Much like creating meaningful "personal books" for your child, you can create your own decodable books that reflect their interests and the phonograms your child has learned. The Raising Robust Readers™ decodable books go from very simple three-word sentences to short chapter books with leveled questions to include comprehension.

6. Blending and Segmenting

Children do not have to memorize all sixteen Single-Sound Consonants before they start blending. They can begin with just three of them. This allows children, early on, to get past the rote learning of individual letters and sounds into *why* they are learning them: to actually *read*.

Those children who are not developmentally ready to blend (put together) and segment (take apart) words will continue to learn individual phonograms. When they are ready, they will have a full toolbox of sounds with which to work on blending and segmenting.

7. Bossy R
er, ur, ir, ear, or, ar

The "r-controlled" phonograms make an /er/ sound. We like to call them the "Bossy R" phonograms. Why? Because, regardless of the vowel, the "r" takes over. The first four Bossy R phonograms (er, ur, ir, ear) teach children that one sound can be spelled different ways which is an essential step for encoding (spelling). The next two "Bossy R" phonograms (or, ar) teach children that a phonogram can have more than one sound. This step will ease children into learning the multiple sounds of consonants and vowels.

8. Multi-Sound Alphabet Letters
c, g, s, x   a, e, i, o, u, y

Here we complete the alphabet. Children now have confidence in recognizing and producing single sounds. Therefore, they are ready to learn multi-sound phonograms, and will be able to do so with more self-assurance and ease. We start with the consonants once again, then go on to the single-letter vowels. Children with Down syndrome are typically literal learners. Teaching all the sounds associated with each of these multi-sound phonograms at once makes it easier for them to understand.

Shari Andress is the National Education Manager for GiGi's Playhouse Down Syndrome Achievement Centers. In her training for new volunteers, she explains, "Children with Down syndrome tend to be literal, or concrete, learners. Teaching all the sounds associated with each of these multi-sound phonograms at once makes it easier for them to understand. For example, if I start with "c" says /k/ and practice only that, it can be very confusing later when I disclose, "Oh, and sometimes 'c' also says '/s/.' When they learn "c" makes two sounds, '/k/' and '/s/,' right from the start, it provides a concrete rule that is always true."

9. The Significant Syllables
Open, Closed, Magic E, Bossy R, Vowel Buddy, Consonant-le.

Syllables are introduced at this point, along with the single-letter vowels, because the syllable type determines the sound of the vowel. Thus, the child not only learns all the sounds of each vowel but *why* each sound has a short, long, or "other" sound. Guessing at a vowel sound is minimized. This is a complex step, so be ready to spend a lot of time here. If your child is not developmentally ready, continue to add the remaining multi-letter phonograms, using them to read and spell words. Continue with creating decodable readers that build on prior phonograms learned and give practice for the new ones.

10. Word Division—Cut the Cake

The guidelines for dividing words into syllables are, not surprisingly, presented in verse form as well...bite by bite. As you will learn in Part 3, "A word is like a birthday cake; it's easier to read if you cut it up in pieces. Just remember you will need..." Check out Chapter 16 to find out what you'll need.

11. The Rest of the Phonograms

At this point, we introduce the remaining phonograms in groups with similarities to help children memorize the sounds. For instance, "Copy

Cat Phonograms" refers to one sound spelled in different ways (oi, oy; aw, au, augh). Presenting phonograms within a context will help children learn and retain their sounds.

TAKEAWAY

Unlike other phonics programs that shy away from teaching individuals with developmental disabilities, Raising Robust Readers™ is designed with these learners at heart. The *unique* multi-sensory sequence of instruction is the hallmark that sets this method apart even from other Orton-Gillingham-based and Science-of-Reading-grounded programs. To ensure consistency and predictability in successful small steps, early blending starts with just two sounds (Single-Sound Consonants + ay) rather than the typical three sounds of C-V-C words. Knowing the six syllable types and their syllable division guidelines enables readers to make the right vowel sound (long, short, other) in words—familiar and unfamiliar.

MY NOTES

....

....

....

....

....

....

....

....

....

....

MOVING FORWARD

We have a wide range of readers, from those who are simply curious to those who are, or will be, teaching phonics to their children. We hope this first part of the book, UNDERSTANDING the Code, has been a benefit to everyone. Next, we will move onto the second part of the book, which will focus on TEACHING the Code to others.

For some, TEACHING the Code will be of the utmost interest. You may be a child's primary reading instructor, either as their parent or school teacher. You may be a parent or teacher who needs more information to advocate at an IEP for your child's reading goals. You may be a homeschooler looking for a more effective approach. Maybe you are not satisfied with the sight-word-only direction your school takes and realize you need to augment your child's instruction at home. Perhaps you need more information to help you make your decision. The next section will be vital for you.

However, even if you have no intention of becoming your child's primary reading teacher, we suggest you at least skim through the upcoming chapters. Even a cursory look will give you a deeper understanding of how all children can develop a strong foundation in reading phonetically. It can help you recognize, and advocate for, your child's potential to go beyond the ABCs and sight words.

We will give you details and examples to help you get started. We do not provide a deep dive into teaching, since this book is an Introduction, not our full-fledged reading program. If you plan to go further, you can investigate Raising Robust Readers™ and other phonics programs to find the one that best reflects Science of Reading principles and matches your needs.

TAKEAWAY

This first part of the book is an Introduction into Understanding the English code. As an overview, it has answers for those who are simply curious about phonics to those who are or plan to teach reading to children with Down syndrome either at home or in the classroom. The Second Part will provide explanations and examples to further your understanding.

MY NOTES

....
....
....
....
....
....
....
....
....
....
....
....
....
....
....
....

Part Three

TEACHING PHONICS the R-IGH-T WAY

Reading ahead will be fruitful even if your child is not developmentally ready for the forthcoming details. Having a foundational understanding of how to teach phonics with phonograms will prepare you for when the time is right.

Going through Part Three will give you insight into fun activities you can easily intertwine in a typical day for *any* activity in daily life. For instance, you could use the "I, We, You" approach (Chapter 6) to teach your child anything from putting on their pajamas to setting the table to riding a two-wheeler bike. In addition, the section on "Assess B, D, A" (Chapter 6) is a good reminder to collect data regarding your child's progress.

Let the fun and the future begin!

Section One
PHONOGRAMS

PHONOGRAMS are single letters (the alphabet) and two (oa)-, three (igh)-, and four-letter (augh) combinations that show just one sound. Generally recognized, there are seventy-two basic phonograms in English.

FEATURES to FOLLOW

While the features below are appropriate for any learner, we gave great thought to those with Down syndrome. As time goes on, these strategies will become more and more natural for both you and your child, and you will be able to spontaneously and meaningfully take advantage of teachable moments in addition to structured learning times.

A Multi-Sensory Approach

Just as it indicates, this is when we use more than one sense in our instructional approach, and our children use more than one sense to learn. We learn and remember best when we create connections through multiple pathways in the brain. The more connections we can make, the better. If we learn something using more than one sense, the information is more likely to stay with us. Hence, we teach each of the phonograms using myriad senses:

- visual—see—printed words and associated pictures
- auditory—hear—jingles set to a familiar tune
- kinesthetic—do—corresponding gestures that illustrate the jingle
- tactile—touch—toy or tiles, and manipulatives

Learner-Centered, Not Curriculum Driven

Although we suggest certain sequences built on our research and experience, the instruction is designed for flexibility to meet your child's individual needs. You may rearrange the order at appropriate times to accommodate your personalized adaptations.

This flexibility also allows you to take advantage of environmental experiences and social activities to facilitate instruction. For example, in November in the United States, it would be a good idea to introduce "th" because it is everywhere: Thanksgiving signs, books, cards, etc. Treat the world like a workbook. The words are all around you, in meaningful places!

Teach On the Go Wherever You Go

You are especially encouraged to use environmental print: menus, signs, books, classroom posters, calendar pages, bulletin boards in the hallway, packaging such as cereal and cookie boxes, etc. For many of our readers with special needs, generalization is a challenge, so teaching the material using environmental print will facilitate this skill. On another practical level, this minimizes the need to create specific worksheets. Besides, finding Keebler® cookies and Cheetos® at the grocery store certainly beats sitting at a desk circling «ee» on non-edible worksheets.

Connect Abstract to Concrete

It is easier for children to learn when we can activate prior knowledge or relate an abstract concept to something known, familiar, or concrete. Although this is true for everyone, it is even more important for our children. As adults, we probably don't remember how we learned about such concepts as letter sounds, time, numbers, etc. We just take it for granted and do it automatically now. But relating these concepts in a step-by-step, concrete manner is essential for our children. For example, compare the sound of a letter (an abstract concept) to the sound of an animal (concrete, known).

I, We, You

Also known as the Gradual Release of Responsibility (Fisher and Frey, 2007), this is a powerful step-by-step approach to help your child learn.

- "I do." You demonstrate the goal using phrases such as, "Watch me," or, "I'll do it first," or, "Let me show you what I mean."
- "We do." Carry this step out together using such directions as, "Let's try this together." You may do hand-on-hand instruction or give oral directions as your child attempts the task.
- "You do." Your child attempts the task independently. Let them know what you expect by using phrases such as, "Now you do

it," or, "Show me how you do it." If your child needs to return to an earlier step, that's fine. This is not a race.

Match, Select, Name

Using letter *h* as an example, here are the three steps.

- Your child will <u>match</u> their *h* card to the card on the table.
- Your child will <u>select</u> the *h* card from a small group of cards with different letters.
- Your child will <u>name</u> the letter *h* when you hold up an *h* card.

Use the I Do, We Do, You Do steps (described above) when introducing this activity. Each step will be repeated as many times as it takes for your child to accomplish the goal. This strategy can easily extend over several days. It is better, in many instances, to teach in small sessions.

Teach; Don't Test

Teach, don't test—until it's time to assess. When you say, "Give me the /p/ card," or, "Sort the big and little letters," you are testing. *Supportive teaching* is neither testing nor doing the same thing as before, only slower and louder—it is interactive, multi-sensory, child-centered teaching. It is explaining, showing, modeling, including, going deeper, backing up to make it clearer, trying a different approach, and giving guidance and hints along the way. Be mindful that the majority of your time is spent teaching. When our children don't seem to grasp the activity, it's always a sign we need to back up and give "sub-step" or "smaller step" instructions to help them.

Assess Progress B, D, A

That said, assessing (testing) is also necessary, before, during, and after instruction. Ongoing assessments tell us where to begin, where to go next, what needs review, and so forth. Assessments can be formal or informal. A trained professional—such as a school reading specialist or independent educational psychologist—can administer formal diagnostic tests. Teachers are required to collect data as they relate to the reading goals on a child's IEP. This data must then be shared with parents so they are aware of their child's progress.

You can also use informal means, such as assessment sheets; personally-created quizzes; pre- and post-tests; and controlled vocabulary stories. Or, you can simply observe and make notes. Documenting progress will give you insight into what to teach and what areas need more support.

Practice Pronunciations

Be sure your pronunciation of sounds is correct. (Appendices D, E, F) For example:

"b": /b/, not /buh/
"d": /d/, not /duh/
"p": /p/, not /puh/

Use air, not "uh." Otherwise, you are adding an additional sound. When it comes time to either decode or encode words, that /uh/ will get in the way. This could be especially problematic for those who still need practice with phonemic awareness and articulation.

Those old pronunciations will not go away easily for you or your child, because, in many cases, they are mispronounced in apps, videos, TV shows, classrooms, and even instructional CDs.

Go to the Raising Robust Readers™ Channel on YouTube to hear the correct pronunciations of the phonogram sounds. Of course, your regional accent will have an effect on your pronunciation.

Sing or Say

To take advantage of teachable moments, you need to be able to spontaneously associate the moment with what you are teaching. Before introducing a jingle (whether published verses, such as those by Raising Robust Readers™, or your own), memorize the lyrics and be familiar with the gestures and associated clues. Then, you are always ready—on the go wherever you go.

It may seem like a lot of memorization, but this is not hard. Give yourself credit. Just think about all those nursery rhymes that still come back to mind. *Mary had a little lamb. Its fleece was white as* _____. See, that was easy.

Names and Sounds Together

When teaching Single-Sound Consonants, use the phrase, "The *name* of the letter is _____. The *sound* of the letter is _____." This is no more confusing than telling your child, "The *cow* says *moo*." It's important to ingrain the idea that the name of the letter is not necessarily the sound it makes. In many instances, especially with later blending and decoding, you may use this phrase to activate memory and allow your child to come up with the sound on their own. In this manner, you help, but you don't provide the answer. Critical thinking is activated.

A Case for Letter Knowledge

We suggest introducing both uppercase (big) and lowercase (little) letters at the same time because both appear at the same time in print, especially environmental print. When doing phonogram hunts, knowing both is especially useful.

If you have taught the concept of size to your child by comparing a big truck and a little truck; a big ball and a little ball; a big chair and a little chair, etc., use this same approach with letters. (We go into this in Chapter 8.)

Concentrate on the lowercase first if your child has trouble learning both simultaneously.

This is a big animal
and a little animal.

This is a big letter
and a little letter.

M m

Get SMART

When establishing goals and objectives for your child, develop SMART goals to provide direction and obtain clear data. Does your child need more varied instruction and practice, or have objectives been met and it's time for new ones?

NOT SMART: "My child will increase their knowledge of phonics."

SMART: "Given specific and explicit instruction on the "ay" and "ee" Vowel Buddy phonograms, [my child] will be able to underline the "ay" and "ee" Vowel Buddy phonograms in ten previously unseen Vowel Buddy word cards with 90 percent accuracy by the end of the first quarter."

Specific - underline "ay" and "ee" in ten previously unseen Vowel Buddy word cards

Measurable - 90 percent accuracy

Achievable - is being given specific and explicit instruction

Realistic - two Vowel Buddies (not six)

Time-bound - by the end of the first quarter

These could be objectives that you write for yourself to help you keep on track, or they can be the formal objectives written on your child's IEP. All IEP goals should be SMART goals.

Skip the Sprint

Above all, always keep in mind that learning to read, for anyone, is a marathon; not a sprint. Our children require patience and practice. They typically require many more repetitions to learn a skill than the average child. If you start to get frustrated, just remember how long and how much practice it took for them to sit up, walk, hold a crayon, tie their shoes. Small doses of instruction repeated over time, rather than single drawn-out sessions, will provide much better results. For both of you! Your becoming sensitive to teaching 'in the moment' will give your child lots of practice. Being perceptive to those teachable moments will provide a lot more fun and require a lot less patience, and hair-pulling, on your part.

TAKEAWAY

- Use a multi-sensory approach - use all the senses to teach
- Be learner-centered, not curriculum driven - focus on your child and individualize instruction
- Sing or say - learn jingles, gestures, etc. to be able to introduce them with ease

- Teach on the go - take advantage of teachable moments wherever you are
- Teach; don't test - spend most of your time teaching, showing, interacting not testing
- Connect abstract - show a connection between abstract and known concepts and objects
- I do, We do, You do - demonstrate, then gradually release support, until your child can do it independently
- Match, select, name - demonstrate first then take small, small steps to mastery
- Names and sounds together - teach both when introducing new letters
- Letter case learning - try both uppercase and lowercase first, then just lowercase if necessary
- Assess - always evaluate progress to determine what has been mastered and what needs to be retaught
- Develop SMART goals

MY NOTES

CHAPTER 7

GETTING STARTED

WHERE DO I START

Begin by assessing your child's knowledge of phonogram names and sounds. This can be as simple as writing down the ones you are aware they know, or you can use a prepared, printed list (Appendices G and H) for assessment sheets.

Once you have completed an assessment, you will know which phonograms (print) your child recognizes and which phonemes (sounds) they can produce correctly. "Correctly" is a rather loose term, in this case. If your child has articulation challenges, it is especially important to continually model correct pronunciations, but accept approximations if they are consistent.

Single-letter vowels (a, e, i, o, u, y) have more than one sound. If your child knows only one of the sounds, mark that as correct, but keep in mind that the sound they know is only part of the multiple sounds that vowel makes, and record that on the assessment.

INDIVIDUALIZE THE ORDER

We suggest introducing phonograms in the order below, but you can individualize the sequence for your child. What is easy or meaningful for your child will differ from what is easy or meaningful for other children.

1. Known Phonograms

To get things going with success, start with the known sounds—typically, some of the alphabet letters. Since your child already knows the sound, they do not have to memorize the jingles and gestures. However, it is a good idea to introduce these jingles with a few mastered letters so your child can begin the new approach with instant success. The pattern will be familiar when they get to those they don't know. It will get your child into the "rhythm" of the instruction. It is a good idea to review the correct sounds for yourself to refine your pronunciation and model correctly. You can listen to the correct pronunciation at the Raising Robust Readers™ website under Resources. https://raisingrobustreaders.com/

2. Easy-to-Pronounce Phonograms

It also makes sense to start with easy-to-produce sounds. An obvious one is Mm (mmmmmm) since your child likely says this when eating ice cream with sprinkles, and you pronounce it when trying to get them to eat their peas. The multi-letter "sh" may seem easy to produce. Holding up your finger to your lips and making a *shush* sound is probably something your child already recognizes. However, for those with low facial muscle tone, "sh" may be difficult. As always each child is an individual, so take advantage of the flexibility of the sequence.

3. Meaningful Phonograms

If your child's name is Piper, then Pp is meaningful. Teach it early on. You can also present a picture of Piper with a name card and phonogram card next to it. Again, you are associating an abstract (name and sound of letter) with a concrete (your child).

4. Continuous-Sound Consonants

Continuous sounds are easy to hear and pronounce. Consonants with continuous sound are f, l, m, n, r, s, v, w and z. These sounds can be "stretched out" and voiced for several seconds until we take a breath.

5. Stop-Sound Consonants

Consonants with stop sounds can be pronounced only momentarily. Have children pay attention to your lips when you teach them. Be careful not to add the 'uh' sound when making these stop sounds. Letters with stop sounds include b, c, d, g, h, j, k, p, q, and t.

ALL AGES—ALL STAGES

As we have said, our readership represents a wide range, from the curious to the classroom teacher. Within that scope, there is also a broad spectrum of developmental readiness for their children. Do not believe that it is too late for your child to read. We know from our own personal experience, from parents, and from GiGi tutors, that adults, even those who do not know the letter sounds, can learn.

In "Debunking Myths: Reading Development in Children with Down Syndrome." *Australian Journal of Teacher Education*, Dr. Kathy Cologon, Macquarie University, writes:

> "Based on research with teenagers and adults who have Down syndrome (e.g. Fowler et al., 1995; Morgan, Moni & Jobling, 2004 & 2009), it can be concluded that as for language development (Abbeduto, Keller-Bell, Richmond & Murphy, 2006), the notion of a 'plateau' or point at which reading development ceases is another myth or 'glass ceiling.'"

Even babies will benefit greatly from songs, conversations, and modeling pronunciations correctly. Songs and gestures on a changing table, bed, highchair, or lap are terrific additions to the natural interaction between baby and parent, siblings, and all those who care. Sing a song. Read a Rhyme. Make the most of baby time.

o-e makes an /ō/.

o-e makes an /ō/.

My friend Joe

stubbed his toe.

oe makes an /ō/.

The upcoming chapters will cover points that are beyond those who are in the early developmental stages. If your child is just beginning on this path, concentrate on the early phases. But do read through all the steps. Learning about more complex strategies ahead of time will give you a head start on knowing when and how to move forward. As you read further, your first reaction may be, "My child can't do this!" But if you do think that, add one more word to the end of that thought:

"My child can't do that **yet**."

TAKE AWAY

After determining which letter names and sounds your child already knows, consider this order for teaching phonograms that are:

- known
- easy to pronounce
- meaningful
- continuous-sound consonants
- stop-sound consonants

It is never too early or too late.

MY NOTES

....

....

....

....

....

....

CHAPTER 8

HOW TO TEACH A PHONOGRAM
With Multi-Sensory Activities

THE SIX STEPS TO SUCCESS

Our *How to Teach a Phonogram* chart (Appendix I) summarizes the six steps to teach phonograms in a multi-sensory manner. We used the "ee" phonogram to "train the brain" to see the two letters as one sound. To illustrate the six steps, we are going to switch over to using the "ay" phonogram for reasons you will soon learn. As you read through the following steps for teaching a phonogram, think of this multi-sensory example as a template for teaching *all* phonograms. By using the same format for each phonogram, you are supporting a propensity toward routine, structure, and the comfort of predictability. Repetition supports these qualities to help your child learn and retain information.

HOW TO TEACH A PHONOGRAM

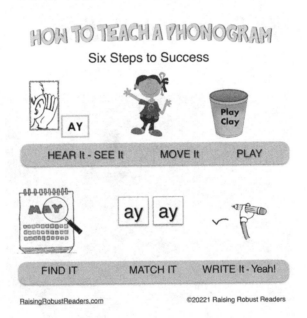

It is important to point out here that the following six steps are not necessarily done in one sitting. Learning a new phonogram can take two minutes, two weeks, or more, depending on your child's developmental level or your busy schedule. You could plan to spend just a few minutes on a playtime activity with a Clue Box item and wind up spending twenty minutes because your child has become so engaged. Or you may have a fun activity planned, but your child is too tired or distracted to participate. So, skip it for now.

After introducing the jingle and gesture, the steps do not have to go in order. You may mix and match them to take advantage of teachable moments.

Why "AY?"

We could have chosen a simple phonogram such as "m" for our example, but we have chosen the "ay" Vowel Buddy phonogram (Appendix J) for several reasons:

1. It reminds us that we read by sounds, not individual letters. Through this method, children learn that a combination of letters has a new name. In this case, the combination of a-y has a new name/sound: ā. Just like children learn that 12 is called twelve, not one-two, they learn to give this combination its proper name. We don't stop at nine when teaching numbers, so let's not stop at Z when teaching sounds and phonograms.

2. This is likely a novel presentation of alphabet letters. We have found that children are eager to learn these new combinations, simply because it's not the "same old, same old" ABCs.

3. The Six Steps (which start below with Step One: Hear it, See it) includes more than just advice on teaching phonograms. They incorporate

vocabulary, fluency, receptive and expressive language, comprehension, and more. As we were developing our jingles, someone remarked that "I see a ray in the bay" may not be a good choice, because there would be many locations that do not have stingrays or bays. We agreed that there certainly are places that do not have stingrays; however, there are probably even more locations that don't have llamas in red pajamas! This is exactly how we build vocabulary and widen experiences: by introducing new words and concepts.

4. Once again, we acknowledge that many of our children experience speech and language delays. Frequent exposure to correct pronunciation is essential. Their repeating the entire jingle is not necessary. Letting your child finish the jingle with you is fine. Also, just because a child cannot say certain sounds doesn't mean they cannot comprehend that phonogram. Even signing a sound, if non-verbal or unintelligible, is a wonderful accomplishment. Take advantage of learning times—like while watching a stingray video—to talk about what's happening. This will help them to practice pronunciation and increase their vocabulary.

5. The "ay" phonogram can be combined with all Single-Sound Consonants to create two-sound words. Even the nonsense words (tay, vay, zay) are important because they prove your child is actually decoding, not just relying on knowing the word already. Because "ay" is always at the end of the word, the structure and repetition facilitate this significant step to reading. m + ay = /m/ + /ā/ = May. This is an excellent way to increase phonological awareness.

6. Our jingles, gestures, and physical associations have been carefully crafted. However, if you wish to use another, more meaningful verse, do so. We applaud those who take the principles and apply them in ways that resonate with their children. Further support phonological awareness by being sure to rhyme correctly with the correct number of beats in your new verse. (I'd like to play. May I stay? A-y makes an /ā/.)

Remember, even babies love hearing the jingles, and toddlers benefit from explanations and questions during reading. All these activities get absorbed and are there in the brain, ready to pull out when the time is right.

MY NOTES

1. HEAR IT, SEE IT

Most children have a natural affinity for music. Even babies will bob and move to a rhythm. So, let's take advantage of this attraction. Singing or saying the phonogram jingles, even to infants, is a powerful way of giving your child opportunities to hear the sounds of our language.

Helping our children *see* language (as we move our finger under the print on the page) while we speak (as we read the words) is powerful. We use the AY page from Raising Robust Readers™ *The ABCs of the Sounds We Read* book to illustrate hearing sounds and seeing them in print. (Appendix J)

- A free color download is available at RaisingRobustReaders. com under "Resources."
- Before discussing the page, watch a video about stingrays from YouTube to create prior knowledge. Since there is a variety, you can pick the one that would be most appropriate for your child.

Remember the Simple View of Reading wherein reading consists of Decoding and Language Comprehension. Talk about the picture. Engage your child in this process just like you do with any picture book you are reading. When you are talking about the picture page to a very young child, you will do all the talking and pointing. Instead of asking questions, you will be describing and explaining. Later, when your child is developmentally able to respond, engage them in the dialogue. Ask lots of questions. For some, signing will be the best choice.

Pediatricians stress the importance of reading books, even to babies. Early exposure to phonemes and phonemic awareness will give them the opportunity to hear individual sounds in our language. (Alas. We wish all pediatricians understood the code and realized that parents can do more than just read *to* their children. Parents are in the best position to show their children *how* to read!)

ay

'a-y' makes an /ā/.
'a-y' makes an /ā/.
I see a ray in the bay.
'a-y' makes an /ā/.

First, using the "ay" page, bring attention to the phonogram "ay" at the top of the page. Talk about what two letters are there. Ask your child to name the two letters. Bring your child's attention to the picture. Ask them: What do you see? Tell me about the colors. What's going on? Who is in the picture? What do you see in the water? If your child cannot verbalize responses, you can describe the images in detail without asking them to answer verbally. If your child is non-verbal, ask them to point in response to your questions or your comments.

Talk about the ray. Point to it as you describe that it's a flat fish with a long tail that moves by flapping its "wings." Point out that this water is called a bay. A bay is a small body of water with land on three sides. This is an opportune time to take a break and sing Raffi's "Down By the Bay" song. If you have the book, bring it out and talk about the bay.

After that break (perhaps, even, the next day), return to the picture and point out the different colors in the text. Bring your child's attention to the red "ay" in the printed jingle, then back to the large "ay" phonogram at the top of the card. This shows that a phonogram is not an isolated symbol. It is part of a larger text and hints at what is to come. Now that you have engaged your child in background information, the picture, and the printed phonogram, begin to sing (to the tune of The Farmer in the Dell) or say the jingle:

> a-y makes an /ā/.
> a-y makes an /ā/.
> I see a ray in the bay.
> a-y makes an /ā/.

Even if you can't sing, just repeating the jingle with its rhyming verse will engage your child. Remember, phonological awareness, of which rhyming is a part, is an extremely important feature in building future readers.

Use the I do, We do, You do method for introducing the jingle above. First, sing it by yourself several times. Move your finger under the words as you do so. Then, invite your child to join you in singing the verse. Of course, many of our children will not be able to do this completely. If your child can sing a few words, praise them for that. If your child is non-verbal, encourage them to sing the song in their head. If your child is deaf or hard of hearing, sign the verse.

"You do" may consist of children simply saying the long-a vowel sound. You would sing the jingle then stop right after "a-y makes an ___" letting your child finish the phrase and say the sound. It is not necessary for your child to repeat the entire verse. This can be a challenging goal for many. Just hearing the verse and finishing with the long "a" sound is a terrific feat.

MY NOTES

2. MOVE IT

Next, let's add movement, giving your child a kinesthetic, or muscle, path for learning and memory: sing/say the jingle; but this time, add the gesture:

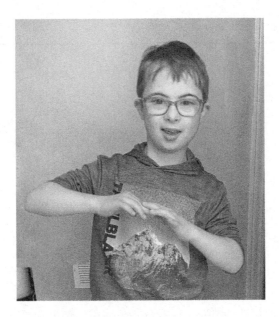

ay **Gesture** (flapping motion) /ā/

With your arms slightly outstretched, and the palms facing down, make gentle "flapping" motions (like a swimming stingray) as you sing, "I see a ray in the bay."

Connect back to the picture by pointing to the side flaps on the ray and reminding your child about the videos and how the ray swims.

Besides adding to multi-sensory learning, gestures add several more layers to our teaching. The most obvious is that it adds fun to the jingle. Would "The Wheels of the Bus" or "Head, Shoulders, Knees, and Toes" be anywhere near as much fun if we just sang the lyrics? We have already indicated that doing a gesture activates another learning modality, but it also gives a more "subtle" memory jog down the road when your child is either decoding (reading) or encoding (spelling) words. It's amazing how quickly they can connect the gestures and the silent clue and produce the sound.

Sometimes, you may not remember to use the gesture. Naturally, we do not recommend flapping your arms while driving in heavy traffic, but, when able, and as long as it is useful, include the gesture and be sure your child is doing it as well. It does not take long for children to master the motions on their own.

You will eventually help your child fade away from using the motions and the songs so that they see the phonogram and say the sound without the props. But at this stage, the jingles and gestures are very important.

MY NOTES

....

....

....

....

....

....

....

....

....

....

....

....

....

3. PLAY

Join the blocks, and build a toy.
'o-i' and 'o-y' both say /oy/.

Now we introduce the Clue Box. Clue Boxes, or Treasure Boxes, hold the playthings or objects that are associated with the jingles. Again, we utilize another pathway, tactile, for learning and retention. A Clue Box may be a container of any shape or material composition, from a wooden box to a colorful canvas tote. Your boxes may be different sizes. For instance, the Single-Sound Consonants Clue Box will be larger because it has sixteen props compared to the Vowel Buddy Clue Box that has seven. As you would suspect, children love to help decorate the boxes. This can be fun and make it super special with your child's personal touch.

We recommend collecting playthings for your Clue Box in this order:

1. <u>Find</u> the object at home
2. <u>Make</u> the item (lots of ideas on the internet)
3. <u>Purchase</u> the item. The internet gives the most choice, but a dollar store saves money.

As expected, when children are allowed to participate in making the choice, at home, at a store, or online, they will be even more connected with the item.

But, naturally, play is not limited to the Clue Box. Playful activities such as making home-made plAYing dough; decorating a trAY; pasting fish and rAYs on a pretty blue bAY, and plAYing baseball reinforce learning. Adjust the activities for the developmental age of your child.

Play is often undervalued. Diane Ackerman, author and Pulitzer Prize finalist, advises, "Play is the brain's favorite way to learn." In our opinion, it is also the adult's favorite way to teach.

MY NOTES

....

....

....

....

....

....

....

....

....

....

....

....

....

4. FIND IT

Phonogram Hunts are so much fun! Point out "ay" in books, of course, but also choose other opportunities to reinforce the presence of "ay" in print all around you: the days of the week on the calendar; PAYDAY® candy wrapper; "ay" on the cup, napkin, and wall of the Subway® shop; and so forth.

Using environmental print is especially important. Our children don't typically generalize information from the desk to the real world on their own, so using the real world is REAL-ly important. Look around the house or classroom. Look all around you. Phonogram hunts can occur in pantries, at the grocery store, at restaurants, on street signs, in the school cafeteria, on the school bus, and so forth. Specific cereals, snacks, sweets with "ay" in the name, and generic words—such as hay, mayonnaise, and playground—provide a phonogram practice session in under a minute. Take pictures of objects or signs while you are out and about, and print them out to make hard copy albums. "Let me see, let me see!" is the typical reaction when kids have their picture taken. Have your child point to the "ay" on a package or sign and take their picture, being sure the phonogram is visible. Create a digital album (good idea for a personal book) for "ay" words so your "phonogram detective" can scroll through and see themselves over and over with "ay."

Teachers can find "ay" in the classroom, in the hallways, on bulletin boards, etc. These are all environmental print, and these all make it possible for our kiddos to connect print with purpose in the real world. These are great to send home as examples for parents.

MY NOTES

5. MATCH IT

At the beginning of this section, we pointed out six reasons we chose "ay" rather than "m" for our step-by-step illustrations. But for this step, we will use "m" because you will start matching uppercase and lowercase with the alphabet letters. If your child already knows both, then you may move on to "ay" and "AY" as well as other multi-letter phonograms. That said, let's move on to the action.

We present both uppercase and lowercase alphabet letters at the same time. We do so because both are present in books and in the environment. Parents and preschools typically introduce the concept of size early. Therefore, if your child understands the concept of a big truck and little truck; big ball and little ball; big chair and little chair, you can use this same approach with letters.

1. Begin the matching process by connecting the abstract (uppercase and lowercase) with the concrete (sets of large and small items). Set out big objects, such as a dog, a cat, a truck, and a book. Give your child a little dog, cat, truck, book. Have your child match the small object to the large object and talk about the difference in size. Use familiar terms like big and little, small and large. Here again, Language Comprehension is woven into our activities.

2. Starting with a familiar alphabet letter (let's say your child knows Mm), put the uppercase phonogram card and the lowercase phonogram card on the table along with the objects. Explain there are big letters and small letters, just like there are big dogs and little dogs, etc.

3. Match the big (uppercase) card to the big dog and the little (lowercase) card to the little dog. Repeat with the other objects. This should go well if you start with an alphabet letter your child knows—at least somewhat. Quick success builds confidence.

4. If your child is starting to match letters, introduce them slowly. (I do) Put just one card on the table and then match the corresponding card. (We do) Help your child to do the same, and finally (You do), ask your child to match the lowercase card in their hand to the uppercase card on the table. Because there is only one card, your child is not only matching independently, but they are matching correctly. Again, we start with success. Our children experience plenty of opportunities to fail. Let's give them plenty of opportunities to succeed.

Continue to use your imagination and create more fun activities. Games are good for matching: Bingo, memory card games, Go Fish, etc. Using dry-erase markers with practice pages in sheet protectors will allow you to use them over and over.

MY NOTES

....

....

....

....

....

....

6. WRITE IT

Handwriting is typically another challenging skill for our children. Like auditory practice, fine motor is another skill to start early and practice frequently. We certainly don't expect our toddlers to produce fine replications of the ABCs, but presenting activities that encourage scribbling, coloring, and making lines, circles, and drawings will get them off to a good start. That is because studies are showing that handwriting is actually very important to the acquisition of language and reading skills. Researchers, using brain scans as well as writing exercises, have concluded that handwriting has a positive effect on memory, retention and activating that part of the brain where language and reading take place.

Sheldon Horowitz, Ed.D., Learning Disabilities Consultant and past Senior Director of Learning Resources and Research at the National Center for Learning Disabilities states, "Some experts believe that forming letters by hand while learning sounds activates reading circuits in the brain that promote literacy." He goes on to advise that, in this prolifically digital age, "Let's give our kids every opportunity to thrive as readers and writers. They can use screens and devices and all sorts of technology. But let's also keep pens and pencils handy. Doing the slow, often difficult work of practicing handwriting can help kids become better readers and writers."

PHONICS THE R-igh-t WAY

This recognizes that our children can play games or use learning apps on devices, but, for those who are capable, this should not be done in place of actually drawing, tracing and writing. Some individuals must use Assistive Technology boards to communicate, but for those who are capable of more, simply pointing to letters on a screen or moving them around to match items in a game on a tablet will not accomplish what actual hand movement will.

Having acknowledged the importance of handwriting, let's look at some suggestions to incorporate writing into teaching a phonogram. Use various media such as finger paints, sidewalk chalk, clay, large pieces of paper, etc. to provide fun and varied experiences. Becky Cabrera likes to match the medium to the phonogram. For instance, clAY. First she forms the letters "A" and "Y," "a" and "y" out of clay, then she dictates a short list of words (May, stay, pray) for her daughter to write in lower-case and uppercase on lined paper.

A large dry-erase board affixed to the wall allows children to stand (or sit in a wheelchair and reach up) to use important large muscles. As always, accept responses as they relate to your child's ability level. Depending on your child's dexterity, letters may be random marks, squiggly snakes, finely reproduced letters on lined paper or a tablet, or anything in between.

But if your child is at a level when they can print, don't include hand-writing corrections when the goal is to determine if your child can "hear the sound and write it down." Wait to focus on that at a separate time. An exception to this may be if your child knows how to form certain letters well but has been sloppy. In that case, have them go back and rewrite the word using the legible representation. Otherwise, make note of letters that need to be practiced and focus on them during handwriting lessons.

Remind your child to say the sound, not the letter name as they write the phonogram for the sound you have dictated. This is another way of using multi-sensory approaches to teach. At first, this step applies to learning individual phonograms. Eventually, you will use the same phrase, "hear the sound; write it down," when your child advances to blending sounds to write words. It is also a good reminder for those children who have a list of spelling words.

MY NOTES

YAY!

Using all six steps means you have used multi-sensory approaches to teach a phonogram. You have included fun. You have responded to your individual child's abilities and learning style. You have taken steps to take your child beyond sight words and the simple ABCs. YAY for YOU and HOORAY for your CHILD!

Your child is learning phonograms with multi-sensory supports: print, jingle, gesture, toys, games, etc. All of these learning supports are useful in learning and retaining the information. All are important in the initial learning stages. Ultimately, however, you want your child to be able to see the phonogram in print and say the sound independently. Over time, you will fade those supports to the point where your child will master seeing the phonogram and quickly produce the sound. "Quickly" will be different for everyone; this is perfectly fine and expected.

For those children who move quickly or already have a foundation in phonogram sounds, you can begin the next steps toward blending. Starting early gives meaning to why sounds are so important. Now, letters have relevance. Now, there is a reason behind why words are pronounced and spelled the way they are. Now, your child can read! Really, really read, not just look at pictures and pretend or guess.

But please, know that even if your child is not ready to blend and begin truly reading, you are still laying a solid foundation with jingles, gestures, and Clue Box treasures. You are learning the logic of English and how our language works so you can pass it on to your child when they are ready.

You are taking your child to a new reading frontier. You are taking them beyond sight words and memorization, guessing, and frustration into a new realm of independent reading. What a gift.

Let me underscore the impact of that gift by sharing part of an email from Cindy Marie Judy, Director of Programs and Volunteers and literacy tutor at the Phoenix GiGi's Playhouse. When updating us on one of her adult students, she wrote, "B had tears when he realized how much it clicked this week and how he had learned so much. His mother was tearing up when he showed her everything after the lesson. And so was I. Very powerful. Thank you for helping me look at things from a different viewpoint."

TAKEAWAY:

The *How to Teach a Phonogram* chart (Appendix I) describes six steps for introducing, teaching, and practicing a phonogram in an interactive way. The steps include:

- Hear it - listen to it pronounced properly
- See it - look at it in print
- Move it - act out a corresponding gesture or action
- Play - demonstrate with a corresponding toy or other object
- Match it - pair with another like it
- Find it - do phonogram hunts to find it in many different places
- Write it - scribble, write, trace, copy, etc.
- YAY.

These six steps apply to all the phonograms. The order can be flexible because the individuality of each child determines which steps take precedence. For instance if your child loves to write, you could move that up after Move it or Play.

Likewise, these steps are not completed, or even attempted, in one sitting. Learning or reviewing a phonogram can take a few moments, a few minutes, a few weeks, or more, depending on each child's developmental level, their interest, their distractibility, or the adult's busy schedule.

MY NOTES

Section Two

BLENDING AND SEGMENTING

Blending is the process of joining sounds to create a word.

Segmenting is the process of separating sounds within a word

CHAPTER 9

SEE the SOUNDS
The Bridge to Blending

"Play gives children a chance to practice what they are learning."

— Fred Rogers, "Mister Rogers' Neighborhood"

Here we begin the transition from learning individual phonograms and sounds to blending those sounds into words.

We suggest this fun activity to help your child understand the difference between "Double e" and "single e."

Make a concrete/abstract connection by creating a fun ice cream activity to explain/review the difference between single and double. This can be an arts and crafts activity using colored construction paper to cut out cone shapes and ice cream scoop shapes. Create a single cone and a double cone with the pieces. Visit https://youtu.be/LGZODejScgc to see a similar ice cream connection. Of course, a trip to the ice cream parlor to illustrate this further is not only instructional, but also rewarding... for both of you. You can extend the language comprehension activity as you enjoy your cones by asking your child if the other customers passing by have purchased a single or double cone. While the craft activity may not be necessary for older children, the trip to the ice cream parlor is still a good idea!

At this time, you, too, are also being "trained" to see that two (or more) letters in words can show one sound. This is very important because the nature of raising robust readers is to bring attention to phonograms and sounds while on the go wherever you go. As adults, we must train ourselves to do this because we are used to reading quickly and not paying attention to the letters that make up the word. Our reading has become automatic, but once we stop and take notice, we can take advantage of those quick teachable moments.

Lory is a literacy tutor at GiGi's Playhouse in New Orleans. She uses Raising Robust Readers™ out and about as well as in her tutoring. She explains, "I've done reading lessons in traffic at red lights with my daughter by breaking down words on street signs. If I had not become aware of phonograms, I would never have been able to do this. After all, a red light doesn't last that long."

The trick is to begin doing your own "solo" phonogram hunts. The sooner *you* familiarize yourself with "Double e" and the rest of the Vowel Buddies, the more automatic it will be for you to see them in words all around you. To be sure, the more you spot these phonograms, the more practice your child will have when you stop in front of a package at the grocery store and proclaim, "I spy 'Double e.' Can you spy 'Double e?'" Now, after purposeful practice, when you look through the market flier at the BOGO items, the word frEE will jump out at you. Try it when you go out next time. "EE" and "ee" abound! (Gradually, as you become familiar with more of the multi-letter phonograms, they will pop out as well.)

Since "ee" is a multi-letter phonogram, you may want to review the *Phonograms Are All Around* song in Chapter 3 and point out that phonograms can have one, two, three, or four letters. With younger or beginning readers, going through the song is fun. If your child is older or further along, just a reminder that a phonogram may have one, two, three, or four letters to show one sound is sufficient.

1. Sing the jingle:
   Double e says /ē/.
   Double e says /ē/.
   It's green I see; it's green I see.
   Double e says /ē/

2. Make the gesture: Put your hand above your eyes, palm down, and look right then left as you sing, "It's green I see; it's green I see. Double e says /ē/."

3. Choose any green object for the connecting clue.

4. Make an "ee" card and head out on a "Double e" phonogram hunt, on the go wherever you go—at home, at school, or out and about.

When you are not on the go, you can use table-time activities such as Match, Select, and Name with "Double e" and "single e" phonogram tiles.

TAKEAWAY

Before children begin to blend and segment words, they need to be able to *see* sounds and *hear* sounds. "Double e" (ee) creates a "bridge" between seeing individual alphabet letters and combinations of letters that make one sound. Children need not read words on this bridge. They just spot the "Double e" in words such as *green, free, greetings, Jeep,* and *street.* If they can repeat the ditty, "Double e says /ē/," that is wonderful, but not essential.

Important note: Adults need to 'train their brain' to see "Double e" all around them so they can help their children. After a while, the kiddos will likely beat you to it.

MY NOTES

CHAPTER 10

HEAR the SOUNDS
Ready to Blend?

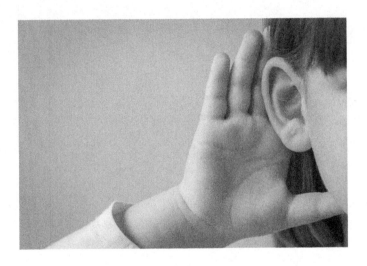

Reading Begins with the Ears

In most cases, you will know if your child is ready to start blending sounds and reading. After all, you would not expect a two-year-old to do so. If you're not sure whether your child is developmentally ready for this big step, try using the exercises below to be sure they understand the concept of words being made up of sounds.

The following sample activities all concentrate on sound. There is no print involved. This lets your child focus on just one thing: sounds (phonemes). It is all about the ability to recognize that words are made up of individual sounds. Oral language, as you remember, typically comes naturally. In most cases, it does not have to be taught. So let's focus on strengthening this more natural skill, if necessary.

Go through the activities to determine if your child can isolate parts (syllables) in words. Of course, we always accept what our children can produce orally if it is consistent. We are not looking for perfect articulation here.

Start with easy (compound words), then go to a little more complicated (two-syllable words, then three-syllable words), then more challenging (sounds within a word). However, if your child cannot do these correctly, this will let you know they would benefit from phoneme exercises before jumping into blending. Practice these and other phonemic awareness exercises (Appendix C), then try again later.

PAT THE PARTS...WITHOUT PRINT

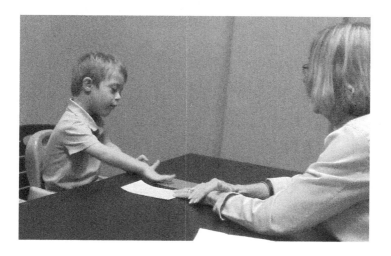

https://youtu.be/awHGvcV_dBM

In the exercises below, we suggest using blank paper squares. We keep the focus on sound, not print.

1. Compound Words

Your child will show they can hear and say the two parts of compound words. If your child is non-verbal, they can just tap the paper. Those children who are deaf or hard of hearing can watch you sign the parts and repeat your gestures.

Materials:

- Three medium-sized blank squares of different-colored, plain construction paper.
- List of compound words such as:
    - For younger children: baseball, highchair, bathtub, sidewalk, cupcake
    - For older children: classroom, homeroom, notebook, bookcase, lunchtime
    - For adults: footprint, railroad, checkbook, freeway

Introduction:

In your own words, geared to your child's receptive level, convey the message that you are going to play sound games in which they will "pat the parts" of words you will be saying. The first game has compound words—long words with smaller words in them.

Instructions:

Sit across from each other with two pieces of plain construction paper between you and your child. This way, your child can see and hear you speak.

- I do: Pat each piece of paper as you say the word "baseball" with a pause between the two parts. Begin by saying the word "baseball." Pat (tap) the first sheet of paper as you say "base." Pat the second piece of paper as you say "ball." Then run your fingers under both squares as you pronounce the whole word slowly. "Base-ball." Be sure you start on the right-hand square, since this is your child's left-hand square from their viewpoint. Repeat this several times.

- <u>We do</u>: With a hand-on-hand motion, have your child imitate the movement and say the names of the two words along with you.

- <u>You do</u>. "That's great—this time, you do it all by yourself. You pat the paper and say the two parts. Then say the whole word by yourself."

Continue with more compound words repeating the I do, We do, You do. When your child demonstrates competency (don't wait for perfection) in hearing and repeating the two parts of the words independently, you can move on to the next "pat the part" activity: Multisyllabic Word Parts.

2. Multisyllabic Word Parts

Next, we move from compound words to syllables within a word. Using the same approach as earlier, explain that the parts you pat in these words are called syllables. Use three pieces of construction paper and a list of familiar, multisyllabic words, such as baby, bacon, jelly, hamburger, banana.

3. Monosyllabic Word Sounds

Now the hard one: hearing sounds within words. This time, use four squares of construction paper and a list of familiar, monosyllabic words with two, three, or four sounds: m-e, c-a-t, h-a-t, c-oa-t, f-ee-t, h-or-se, t-r-ai-n, t-r-ee-s .

Follow the same format that you presented previously beginning with I Do. Begin by slowly saying the word, "coat." Then pat (tap) the first sheet of paper as you say /c/. Pat the second piece of paper as you say, /ō/. Pat the third piece of paper as you say /t/. Then run your fingers under the three squares as you pronounce the whole word slowly: "coat." Be sure you start on the right-hand square, since this is your child's left-hand square from their viewpoint. Repeat this several times.

Start with familiar two-sound words, since hearing the separate sounds within a word is more difficult.

HEARING CONCERNS

There is a difference between being ready for the concept of blending sounds and being able to hear sound differences. Dr. Cronin, who is also the mother of a son with Down syndrome, states, "It is difficult for children, perhaps particularly children who have Down syndrome, to let you know they are having hearing problems, especially if they are mild." Have your child's hearing checked with an audiologist if you have suspicions. If there are hearing problems, you will learn if there is a general hearing loss or specific sounds that are affected. You can then work with a speech pathologist on specific therapies.

MOVING AHEAD

These exercises also benefit children who start to blend two-sound words and later have difficulty decoding or encoding more sounds. Go back to these exercises to bring awareness to hearing sounds.

TAKEAWAY

Before starting blending exercises, check to see if your child can hear individual parts of words. Use activities without print to check their ability to hear separate sounds, from separating compound words to "patting out" sounds within a word.

If parents suspect there is a hearing problem, it is advisable to have a thorough test with an audiologist.

As important as it is to hear and say sounds correctly, children who are deaf or hard of hearing can learn to read phonetically. The kinesthetic use of sign language shows the learner that sounds have a letter and letters have sounds.

MY NOTES

CHAPTER 11

<u>SAY</u> the SOUNDS
Beginning to Blend

"The kindest thing you can do for a beginning and struggling reader is to give them the time and encouragement they need to grunt and groan their way through sounding out words. You're rewiring their brains, and it's hard work."

— *Dr. John Shefelbine*

TO BEGIN

The manner in which we introduce blending is unique to our sequence of instruction. As previously mentioned, we do not start with short vowel sounds represented by single-letter vowels. Drilling our children with /ă/ words in a consonant-vowel-consonant (C-V-C) pattern (like cat, map, and dad) would be fine if it were not for words like m-a-y, w-a-r, w-a-s, and countless others. Instead, we begin blending with vowel sounds that stay consistent. We use the same C-V-C pattern, but we use the seven long-sound Vowel Buddies so we don't have to explain why "may" says "may," not mmm-ah-yuh. Our children require consistency and predictability. This unique sequence provides both.

You may begin blending after your child learns three Single-Sound Consonants and the "ay" Vowel Buddy . This allows you to start creating words with just two sounds. Doing so at this stage will allow children to understand why they are learning phonograms: to read, to write, and to spell. This is especially important if children are older.

Children continue to learn additional phonograms as they work on blending. In this manner, they expand their reading experience.

Moving from learning individual phonograms to putting sounds together and separating sounds is a challenging leap; it is much more cognitively complex. Some children catch on rather quickly, but most will need much practice.

This holds true for children in general, but, with few exceptions, it will take even more time for those with Down syndrome. If you know this beforehand, you can be prepared for this phase and not give up. Compare it to the other areas where your child took extra time, instruction, and practice. Crawling? Walking? Tying shoes? Counting? Dressing? Potty training? Think of the various challenges your child overcame, and keep them in mind as you come to plateaus.

As progress occurs, fade away using the multi-sensory supports that were so important in learning the phonograms and move your child toward seeing and saying the sound quickly.

BLENDING WITH PHONOGRAM TILES

The following is a brief description of how to teach blending using phonogram tiles. (Go to the Raising Robust Readers™ Channel on YouTube. com to see the video.)

We used "ee" to begin "training the brain" to *see* sounds in words. Now we go to the next stage—a huge one—where you will help your child *say* those sounds in words.

We use Single-Sound Consonant tiles and begin with Vowel Buddy "ay." We start with "ay" for several reasons:

- "Ay" makes the long-a sound. Children are used to saying this sound since it is the name of the first letter of the alphabet. Hence, we are starting with familiarity.

- "Ay" is consistent and predictable. Unlike the single vowel "a," which has three sounds, "ay" represents only one sound.

- "Ay" comes at the end of base words. Again, we are presenting a word pattern that is consistent and predictable, playing right into our children's personalities.

- You can add all sixteen consonants, one by one, to "ay" and make words. Some will be nonsense words, but they are also important since blending the sounds correctly proves they are not just reading them because they are already familiar with the word. They will prove your child is really blending with confidence.

Once your child is proficient with the "ay" Vowel Buddy, go back and repeat the process with the "ee" phonogram. They are already familiar with "ee," since you used it to "train the brain." See Appendices K and L for a list of two-sound and three-sound Vowel Buddy words to use after "ay" and "ee."

To Begin:

Model the sounds correctly. Be sure not to add the /uh/ sound. Accentuate the air. Especially for those children with speech and language delays, frequent exposure to correct pronunciation is essential.

Directions:

1. Line the consonant tiles your child knows at the top of a mat on a desk or table. Place the "ay" tile toward the bottom of the mat.

In your own words, tell your child that this is an exciting game. They are going to learn to read words. They are becoming a real reader!

Remember one of our favorite phrases: *"Teach, don't test."* This is a teaching session. You should give as much support and as many clues as necessary. This is not cheating. This is teaching.

Begin by pointing to each of the tiles and have your child give you the sounds. This does several things:

- It's a good warm-up for your child;
- It reminds them that you are focusing on sounds. If they say the name instead of the sound, use the phrase, "The name of the letter is _____; the sound of this letter is _____."
- It lets you know which phonograms your child doesn't remember. When your child hesitates too long, you will know you will need to practice that phonogram some more. Avoid these tiles during the blending lesson. You want to start with the ones they know so it increases the chances of success.

2. Start by pointing to the "ay" tile and asking what sound that phonogram makes. When your child responds correctly, praise them.

Then explain, in your own words, that you are going to bring down one of the consonant phonograms. Start with any sound your child can pronounce easily, consistently, and correctly. Now begin the instruction, using I do, We do, You do. Move down the "m" (or whichever) tile. Then slide the tile close to the "ay" tile. As you slide the "m" tile to the right, pronounce the sound /mmmmmmm/. When the "m" tile touches the "ay" tile, say /ā/. Repeat this several times. Running your finger under the two tiles, left to right, connect the two sounds together so it sounds like the completed word "may." Repeat this exercise several times.

When you finish with the "m" tile, replace it and bring down another consonant.

Repeat the process with a new consonant sound. Fade away the *I do, We do* as soon as your child shows they understand what you want. Move onto You do: let them do the format several times independently until they get the word right.

Hear the Sound and Pull it Down

As your child progresses, add these activities:

- You say a sound. Your child finds the correct tile and moves it down toward the bottom of the mat. You both continue with additional sounds and tiles until the word is completed. Have your child read the word. (p-l-ay)
- You say a word, and your child finds the phonogram tiles and pulls them down to spell out the word.
- Your child says a word, pulls down the tiles they need, makes the word they chose, and reads it.

Here are some tips for decoding longer words:

- While blending sounds from left to right may be better, adding each sound in order, children do not always have to start on the left and go sound by sound to the right. Sometimes it is easier for children to begin with the multi-letter phonogram they recognize. For example, the word "feet."

- Children may start in the middle, move to the left, blend those two sounds, then add the final sound before saying the whole word.
  - ee (middle)
  - fee (left-initial)
  - feet (right-final)

Or, they may start in the middle, move to the right, blend those two sounds, then add the initial sound before saying the whole word.
- ee (middle)
- eet (right-final)
- feet (left-initial)

TAKEAWAY

Instead of beginning to blend with the typical consonant-short vowel-consonant pattern, it is less confusing and frustrating to begin with a long vowel phonogram that does not have multiple sounds. To make it even easier, we start with just two sounds, not three. This way, we take small steps and build skill, confidence, and success in this big leap to reading. By adding "ay" to the end of the Single-Sound Consonants, children can start to build and read using a consistent, reliable, predictable pattern. Going to "ee" next uses a familiar phonogram. Children can add additional letters and read longer words: *fee, feet, fleet*

JUDY O'HALLORAN & MARILEE SENIOR

MY NOTES

SELECT the SOUNDS
Two-Sound Consonants

Once your child has learned Single-Sound Consonants and Vowel Buddies with one sound, introduce Two-Sound Consonants *c*, *g*, *s*, *x*. Children do not have to memorize all sixteen consonants and seven Vowel Buddies before being introduced to multi-sound consonants. If they have been confidently reading and spelling words with "one-choice" sounds, they are ready to learn the multiple-sound consonants.

Remember, connecting a new concept with prior knowledge and the concrete is important. Explain to your child at their level, that, so far, each phonogram has made only one sound. But some make more than one sound. Just like a dog, cat, or person can make more than one sound, so can a phonogram. Make it fun. If you need to ask the questions and model the answer yourself, that's fine.

> You: "The puppy says, 'Hi.' What sound does he make?"
>
> Child: (Makes a barking sound.)
>
> You: "The puppy is mad. What sound does he make?"
>
> Child: (Growls.)
>
> You: "Oh, the puppy got hurt. What sound does he make?"
>
> Child: (Whines.)

A Grrrrreat Explanation for Multi-Sound Phonograms

A dog usually <u>barks.</u>

Sometimes a dog will <u>growl</u>.

Sometimes a dog will <u>whine</u>

GETTING STARTED

Of course, these multi-sound phonograms are taught with jingles, gestures, and clue-box items just like the Single-Sound Consonants and Vowel Buddies. Here is a sample for the consonant "c":

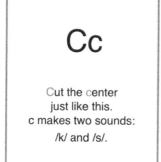

Follow the same teaching format as before. The gesture may include 1) a motion with two fingers like cutting with scissors as you sing "cut"; and 2) touch the center of your palm with the forefinger of the other hand as you sing "center." The Treasure Box would include a pair of children's or play scissors and a piece of paper with a hole in the center. After your child knows the two sounds, work toward just saying, "C makes two sounds: ____and ____." Pause and let your child finish by saying the two sounds.

Continue to use the *How to Teach a Phonogram* chart to teach the remaining Two-Sound Consonants.

SAMPLE ACTIVITIES

Play games to hear the difference in sounds:

Phonogram Sound Hunt:

Materials:

- A pair of children's scissors and a piece of paper with a hole in the center.
- Pictures of /k/ car, cup, crown, corn, castle, etc.
- Pictures of /s/ items: celery, circle, cent, cell phone, cereal, etc.

Directions:

Talk about all the different pictures to be sure your child knows what they are. Be sure to emphasize the /k/ and /s/ sounds. Put the correct sound card next to it. After you have demonstrated this, choose one picture at a time and have your child match the correct sound card.

For more active learning, hide the picture cards around the classroom, house, or play area, and when your child finds each, have them pronounce the words. We know pronunciation will be difficult or impossible for some children. They can instead match the phonogram card to the picture, or they can sign the /k/ or /s/.

For more fun, include some active play and emphasize the sounds:

- Cut celery
- Fill cups with different colored crayons
- Make a sand castle
- Count five cents
- Talk about different cereals in the supermarket aisle, etc.

Help your child remember the sounds in order. This is important because they appear in the jingle in the order of the frequency they are pronounced in words. However, if your child can easily repeat the sounds out of order, and does so after a few attempts by you to get them in the correct order, don't worry about it. It's more important to have them master the sounds. Continue to use the Six Steps to Success on the *How to Teach a Phonogram* chart to teach each Two-Sound Consonant.

These four Two-Sound Consonants (c, g, s, and x) are a good segue into learning the multiple sounds of vowels, which are coming up next.

TAKEAWAY

Some consonants (c, g, s, x) can make more than one sound. Children have experienced much consistency. Their continuous progress leads to stronger confidence. Children are ready to learn and remember two sounds for one consonant through simple jingles, gestures, and play.

MY NOTES

....

....

....

....

....

....

....

....

....

....

CHAPTER 13

<u>HEAR</u> the SOUNDS

Vowels a, e, i, o, u...y

Finally! The vowels! The single-letter alphabet vowels, with all their sounds!

It may seem counterintuitive to wait so long to work on these single-letter vowel sounds. After all, children's books and classroom readers are full of these words. Isn't that why we teach them right away?

But we are fitting the program to the child, not the child to the program—or to the books, or to a school-district calendar.

You might think, "But it will take so long before we reach this point. I want my child to be able to read books like the other kids."

Well, Judy was in the same boat as you are now. She wanted Casey to talk as soon as her other boys had talked, be able to add numbers like all the other first graders, and ride a two-wheeler like all the other third-grade neighborhood kids. But that didn't happen. And he certainly didn't learn to read like "the other kids" by being given books he couldn't understand and instructions that didn't give him the opportunity to learn.

May we remind you that two-thirds of "those other kids" in fourth and eighth grade read below proficiency? That's nothing to wish for. Perhaps that percentage would be different if they had been given smaller, more logical steps.

Granted, beginning books are loaded with a, e, i, o, u, and y vowel words, but they also have Vowel Buddy words and Bossy R words. Take time to select books such as *Sheep in a Jeep* (and all the other *Sheep* books by Nancy Shaw). *No Sleep for the Sheep!* by Karen Beaumont is another great source for shared reading, decodable words, vocabulary, and fun. Popular children's books are not typically written with controlled vocabulary (lots of words your child can decode). However, it is important to expose children to their rich language and images. You definitely want to read them to/with your child for modeling and enjoyment. The bonus is that eventually, with patience, your child can acquire the skills to read them independently.

If your child is older and has had some success with traditional reading programs but is now plateauing, this chapter is an excellent place to begin instruction. We are learner-focused, not curriculum-driven, so do what is best for you and your child. If they have not received phonogram instructions previously, fill in those unknowns as you come across them.

Memorizing the multiple sounds of each vowel is the first step. From there, our children need to know which sound to use. Here, we introduce learning the types of syllables because syllable types tell us which sound the phonogram represents. For most parents, this is a real game-changer. Now parents and teachers have a simple process that explains when to make the long, short, or other vowel sound.

Our children may start out well in school, because they look at pictures or memorize words and appear to be reading. But typically, the gap begins to widen when they reach second or third grade, when there are too many unique words to memorize and not enough pictures to help.

If our children can't read the words, they can't comprehend the message. And *comprehension* is what reading is all about. The fact is, our children are not reading at a particular grade level if they cannot comprehend what they are reading at that level. Unfortunately, the gulf will widen as the years pass—unless we give them a foundation to decode unfamiliar words.

IDENTIFYING VOWELS

Your child should be able to identify and name the six single-letter vowels by this point. In the ABCs song, all letters are lumped together without reference to their being consonants or vowels. It's important, however, to know the difference because you will use these terms—*consonants* and *vowels*—a lot, especially when dividing words into syllables.

When introducing or using the terms "vowels" and "consonants," keep it simple. Children only need to memorize the six vowels, because all the rest are consonants.

Just as you have made concrete/abstract connections previously, do so again to show there is a difference between vowels and consonants. For example, you could introduce the terms by making a small pile of colored markers and a larger pile of crayons. As you point to the markers, tell your child, "We call these 'markers.'" Then, point to the crayons and explain, "We call these 'crayons.'" Make a pile of the vowel letter tiles face down next to the markers, and a pile of consonant letter tiles next to the crayons. Then, pointing to the first collection, say, "We call these 'vowels.'" Pointing to the other stack, say, "We call these 'consonants.'" Then, invite your child to find out what letters are in the vowel pile.

No surprise here—we have a little ditty to teach the vowels. It goes to the tune of "Bingo Was His Name."

a, e, i-o-u.

a, e, i-o-u.

a, e, i-o-u.

And sometimes even y.

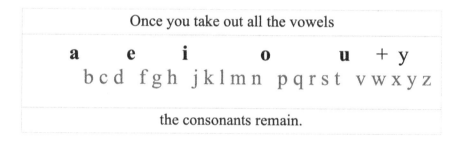

Once you take out all the vowels

a   e   i   o   u   + y

b c d   f g h   j k l m n   p q r s t   v w x y z

the consonants remain.

LEARNING THE VOWEL SOUNDS

Oo

Hop, go into
circles like I do.
o has three sounds:
/ŏ/ /ō/ /oō/.

Oo /ŏ/ /ō/ /oō/

Hop, go into.

Although children learn the vowel names in a, e, i, o, u, y order, you do not have to teach them in that same sequence. In our experience, children really have fun with the action that goes with the "o" vowel. Have your child learn the jingle.

(To the tune of "Twinkle, Twinkle Little Star")

Hop, go into
Circles like I do.
O makes three sounds:
/ŏ/ /ō/ /oō/

Draw three circles on the driveway, then have them say /ŏ/ as they hop into the first, then /ō/ as they jump into the second, then finally /oō/ when they reach the third circle.

Learning the A Vowel Sound

"A" is a common vowel sound. When teachers give instruction on consonant-vowel-consonant words, they often begin with the short "a" vowel. So, we feature "a"—with all its three sounds—as our example.

Abby ate almonds
that taste blah.
"A" makes three sounds:
/ă/ /ā/ /ah/.

"A" Sample Activity

Your objective is to have your child match the items to the correct sounds of "a."

Materials:

- Phonogram "a" card
- An apple
- An apron
- A bag of almonds (or a picture if there is an allergy issue)

Directions:

Put an apple, apron, and almond on the table. Discuss each one emphasizing the different "a" sounds of each. In your own words, present the exercise as follows:

I do:

I am going to say the first sound of the phonogram "a" /ă/; then I will point to the object that starts with that sound of "a."

We do:

Let's say the first sound of the phonogram "a" together /ă/, and you can help me pick up the item that starts with that sound. Give any assistance, verbal and/or physical, that will help your child pick up the apple.

You do:

I will say the first sound of the phonogram "a" /ă/. Then, you will pick up the correct item all by yourself. (If the choice is incorrect, you will choose the correct one and instruct/discuss the sound more.)

Repeat with the apron /ā/ and then the almonds /ah/.

Note: You can substitute any high-interest objects that represent the three sounds in these activities.

MY NOTES

THE "UH-MAZING SCHWA

ə

/uh/

Vowels make long and short sounds. Well, duh—we know that! But what you might not know is that all vowels *also* make another sound, called the schwa sound. It sounds like the "uh" in the "duh" word above, and may appear as an upside-down e symbol /ə/ when written phonetically.

The formal term "schwa" doesn't tell us much, so if we use the term "lazy vowel," we can help our children understand.

Let's back up a bit. In spoken language, we speak with words that have many syllables; but we do not say them slowly and distinctly enough to pronounce every word with great clarity. In each word we speak that has two or more syllables, a stressed syllable is louder or stronger than the other/s. In the unstressed (weaker) syllables, we often use an "uh" sound rather than the distinct vowel sound. Again, we note that different parts of the country have different accents, so these may be pronounced differently—use words that work for your regional accent, if these do not.

- ə bout
- ə lec tric

- di nə saur
- də plo mə

SPELLING AND WRITING PRACTICE

Using the "uh" sound is normal when we are talking, but when it comes to spelling these words, schwa sounds can add an extra challenge. We don't spell words using an upside-down /ə/ (the schwa symbol), so which vowel do we use when we hear that sound?

One strategy for older children is using word banks to help build visual memory. If your child has difficulty spelling a word with the schwa sound, have them practice reading that word so they get used to seeing it spelled correctly. Then, have them write the word on a card, paying particular attention to the vowel being used. Accumulate these words and practice them from time to time.

TAKEAWAY

It seems counterintuitive to wait so long to introduce vowels when single-letter vowels are in the vast majority of printed words. However, we are looking at the big picture here, going from simple concepts ("igh" says /ī/) to more complex concepts ("i" makes three sounds: / ĭ/, /ī /, /ē /. Going slowly and connecting the abstract (sounds) with the concrete (physical objects) or familiar (animal sounds) allows children to first learn the sounds and then, more importantly, know *when* to use which sound.

We make the program fit the learning needs of the children. We don't make the children fit the program. In fact, if your child's school is using the traditional approach, concentrate on this chapter after reading through the whole book (and filling in with essential information like multi-letter phonogram sounds).

The "uh-mazing" schwa is also introduced and explained.

MY NOTES

Section Three
SYL-LA-BLES

This is where independent reading reaches reality.

Buckle your seat belts. The flight
is about to take off.

CHAPTER 14

THE SIX SILLY SYL-LA-BLES

SYL-LA-BLE SIGNIFICANCE

Here we are at the next quantum leap!

If you looked at the title "Reading Syllables" and thought that this section would not be relevant to you because your child is too young, we are glad that you kept reading because you will learn that these chapters are important for you...for now and later.

Just as you sang the ABCs song long before your child began learning individual letter names and sounds, you can do the same with the Six Silly Syllable jingle. Even preschoolers sing the song just as enthusiastically as they do "The Wheels of the Bus." You can sing the song and do the gestures with your child long before they are ready for actual syllable instruction. Later, when your child is ready, they will already be familiar with the names. What a bonus!

As you continue to read, you will learn why words sound the way they do. For instance, "Why does diner say *diner*, when dinner says *dinner*?" You probably don't think about that as an adult, because you are a proficient reader and know how to pronounce each. You don't have to figure that out. But an emerging reader, especially one who has been drilled and drilled on the short "i" sound, will wonder *why* they aren't both pronounced *dinner*.

After reading this section, you will be able to explain and show your child the reasons *why* in meaningful, understandable ways. You are able to help your child study words and read them correctly. You no longer have to resort to, "I don't know why it says that. English is crazy. Just memorize it."

Recently, we saw a post from a teacher proclaiming how she taught 600 sight words in first grade. We are not opposed to meaningful sight words in first grade, but our immediate thought was, "Why?" Why memorize 600 sight words when you can open up the whole world of independent reading with just seventy-two basic phonograms and the six syllable types? Remember, we are not opposed to sight words when memorized for meaningful purposes, but in this book, we give you an alternative—in a fun-filled, flexible, individualized, child-centered manner.

In Chapter 10, you had your child pat the parts of a word to determine if they could hear the number of syllables, but syllables are far more than beats in a word. Syllables tell the word what to say. When we take the time to help our children understand how words work, we remove many of the stumbling blocks they encounter and turn them into stepping stones. We hope you'll take a look, even if your loved one isn't yet ready. Because one day soon, they will be.

TAKEAWAY

Syllable knowledge creates a quantum leap in independent reading. That is because the type of syllable tells us what the vowel sound says: long, short, or other. For this reason, our sequence pairs vowel knowledge with syllable knowledge. Every syllable has to have a vowel, and every vowel has to know what sound it is supposed to make.

MY NOTES

....

....

....

....

....

....

....

....

....

....

....

....

....

....

....

....

SYL-LA-BLE TYPES

There are six syllable types, and, similar to teaching the seasons of the year, we introduce them, by name, all together. Then we focus on teaching the features of each, one at a time. Like blending, this is typically a long process, so be patient.

As you know by now, the best way to begin is with a song. This time it's "The Six Silly Syllables" song. It would be more accurate to name it "The Six *Significant* Syllables," but "Silly" is a fun word and a heck of a lot easier to say or sing than "significant!"

Before introducing this jingle, tell your child the song is about syllables. Explain that syllables are parts of words. There are six kinds of syllables, and each one has a name. Review the "pat the parts" game with compound words from Chapter 10—this is an excellent way to associate the word "syllable" with the concept of "parts." You might want to introduce this exercise here if you skipped it earlier.

Memorize the lyrics and gestures of the jingle beforehand so you can guide your child through the song. After singing the song with your child several times, model the gestures that go with the syllable types.

(to the tune of "Let Your Ears Hang Low")

Use your hands and sing along with me.
The six silly syllables are so easy:
Open, Closed, Magic e,
Bossy R, Vowel Buddy, Consonant -l-e.

Open	Closed
Magic e	Bossy R
Vowel Buddy	Consonant -le

When you get to the place in the verse where you say each syllable name, make the corresponding hand gesture as illustrated in the pictures above. They add instructional value, and, like the motions in "Itsy, Bitsy Spider," "Five Little Monkeys," and "If You're Happy and You Know It," they make the song more fun to sing. Your child may not be able to say all these terms. That is fine. You will sing/say the jingle and help your child do the gesture as you say the syllable name.

Once again, it is important to have associated gestures. In the future, when dividing words into syllables, you can use the gesture as a hint if your child gets "stuck." It is incredible how quickly the connection is made without saying anything. It's a wonderful, gentle reminder that is subtle and very effective.

TAKEAWAY

Learning all syllable types at once is like learning the names of all four seasons at once. Details of each season come later—one at a time. So it is with syllables.

Children can even learn this song when they are very young. Just like they probably don't know what a dell is in "The Farmer in the Dell," they don't need to know what "closed" means yet. The bonus is that they will already know the names when it comes time to learn the details.

MY NOTES

....

....

....

....

....

....

....

....

....

CHAPTER 15

TEACHING ONE TYPE AT A TIME

VOWEL BUDDY SYLLABLES

Now let's move on to learn about the individual syllable patterns. We start with the Vowel Buddy syllable because your child is familiar with the term. They have progressed from Vowel Buddy phonograms to Vowel Buddy words to Vowel Buddy phrases, sentences, and, perhaps, homemade Vowel Buddy decodable readers. As such, identifying Vowel Buddy syllables is a simple step forward. The term will be familiar before you go on to the more complex syllables "open" and "closed."

You will take the characteristics of a Vowel Buddy syllable described in the graphic below and put it in your own words that your child can understand.

Vowel Buddy Syllables

feet   right

In the **Vowel Buddy** syllable where two vowels are found, together they will make just one vowel or vowel-like sound.

The multi-letter phonograms with gh at the end are in vowel buddy syllables. 'GH' is a silent friend.

Focus first on monosyllabic words such as nail, light, freight, etc. to keep it simple. If your child has expressive language challenges, they don't need to read the words aloud. Pointing or sorting shows your child understands.

In the last chapter, we presented the syllable song and gestures which address all six syllables. But since this book is an introduction, not a complete teaching manual, we do not go into details for *all* syllable types. We touch on three of the six to get you started.

The suggested activities below should help you demonstrate the Vowel Buddy syllable in ways your child can understand.

Suggested Activities

Since this is a new concept, your child may benefit from Match, Select and Name, and I do, We do, You do when introducing these activities.

1. Create a list of Vowel Buddy words your child knows. Write them on index cards. Make another set with single-vowel words. The goal is to have your child see the Vowel Buddy syllable pattern and pick those words.

2. If possible, laminate cards so you can reuse them. Mix the cards and pick a few at a time. Ask your child to pick out the cards that belong on the Vowel Buddy syllable team. If they hesitate, have them underline the Vowel Buddy phonograms with a dry-erase marker on the laminate. When our children don't seem to grasp the activity, it's always a sign we need to back up and give "sub-step" or "smaller step" instructions to help them.

3. Grab a safari hat and join your child on Vowel Buddy syllable hunts. These will be like the Vowel Buddy phonogram hunts described in Chapter 8 "Find it." But now you are searching for syllables.

(Tip: Go to Bossy R syllable next since this is also a familiar term and use the same format.)

MY NOTES

....

....

....

....

....

....

....

....

OPEN then CLOSED SYLLABLES

OPEN SYLLABLE	CLOSED SYLLABLE
nō	nŏt
At the end of an **open** syllable, no consonant is found. The vowel at the end will say its name and make a long vowel sound.	In a **closed** syllable, the vowel is short 'cause a consonant closes it in. This syllable has just one vowel and a consonant at the end.

Open and closed syllables are more complex. Unlike Vowel Buddy and Bossy R, these open and closed wordings are likely new for your child. Spatial terms are often difficult for children with Down syndrome. Yet again, we address not only Decoding skills, but Language Comprehension as well. Before introducing the syllables one at a time, you will introduce spacial terms that apply to both. For example, it's hard to explain open without comparing it to closed:

1. Begin by going over, explaining, and demonstrating spatial words: open, close, in, end, long, short, over, under, etc.

2. Use physical objects to create the concrete/abstract connection such as various lengths of ribbon to discuss long and short. Or an activity such as having your child stand *next to* a big cardboard box; *behind* the box; get *in* the box, *close* the top flaps of the box; *open* the top flaps of the box.

3. Use multi-sensory activities like the one below to help your child further understand these concepts. While they are so obvious to us, they are abstract concepts for many of our children.

OPEN SYLLABLES

At the end of an **open** syllable,
No consonant is found.
The vowel at the end will say its name
And make a long vowel sound.

Suggested Activities

Use the suggested activities for the Vowel Buddy syllable as a guide.
Sample words:
he; be; hi; go; me; no; etc.

CLOSED SYLLABLES

In a **closed** syllable, the vowel is short
'Cause a consonant closes it in.
This syllable has just one vowel
And a consonant at the end.

Suggested Activities

Use the suggested activities for the Vowel Buddy syllable as a guide.
Sample words:
hem; bet; hip; got; met; not; etc.

OPEN and CLOSED

Here is one activity to help your child understand open and closed syllables together.

Materials:

1. Make a house out of construction paper with a door that will open and close.
2. Write a consonant on the door. (If you laminate the house, you can use a dry-erase marker. If not, use sticky notes to change the consonant on the door.)
3. Open the door so your child cannot see that consonant.
4. Sample word pairs: he/hem; be/bet; hi/him; go/got

Steps:

Remember the difference between teaching and testing. At first, you will use I do and We do to introduce the concept of open and closed syllables. Then go to You do. Using the example above, ask:

> _You:_ What kind of syllable is this?
> _Child:_ Open syllable.
> _You:_ Why?
> _Child:_ Ends with a vowel.

You: What sound does the vowel make?
Child: Long. /ē/
You: Could you read it with the long e sound?
Child: He.

"I am going to *close* the door."
Close the door with the consonant showing.

You: What kind of syllable is this?
Child: Closed syllable.
You: Why?
Child: It has one vowel. It ends with a consonant.
You: What sound does the vowel make?
Child: The short vowel sound. /ĕ/
You: Could you read it with the short e sound?
Child: Hem.

Open		Closed		
b	e	b	e	t
g	o	g	o	t
h	i	h	i	t

Phonogram tiles are a great tactile activity to help your learner understand how the vowel sound changes. (Appendix L)

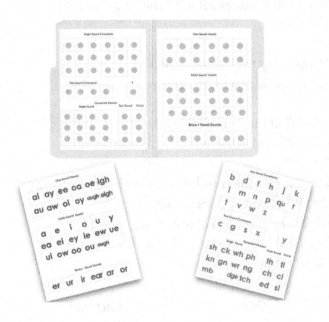

Assess Progress

Keeping data is important for tracking your child's learning. To assess
your child's progress, especially if you are a homeschool parent, write out
objectives in the form of SMART goals. SMART goals stand for Specific,
Measurable, Attainable, Realistic*, and Timely*. (See Chapter 6 to review
the SMART parts.) *Relevant and Time-Bound terms are also used.

Extended Practice

Now that you are introducing your child to syllables, you can use shared
reading with a typical children's book or other print material to generalize this skill. Since your child has not yet learned how to divide syllables,
you will pick out words with easily recognizable syllables like "highway."
Cover "way" and have your child read "high." Then cover "high" and have
your child read "way." Uncover both and have them read the whole word.

Do the same thing with words that have only one Vowel Buddy syllable such as appears in this sentence: "The green pails contain three boats." Let's say your child is having trouble with the word "contain." Cover "tain" and (you) read "con." Then cover "con" and ask your child what kind of syllable is showing. When they reply it is a Vowel Buddy syllable, have them read it. Uncover "con" and read "contain" together.

This is a powerful transition as they learn to identify the remaining types of syllables. In the next chapter, you can give your child even more power—the ability to look at a multisyllabic word and figure out how to break up the word into syllables by themselves.

TAKEAWAY

After learning the Six Silly Syllable song, the next step is to learn the characteristics of each syllable. This is important because each syllable type has control over the sound of the vowel/s in that syllable. We do not follow the sequence in the song. Instead, we start with the Vowel Buddy syllable because children can use their prior knowledge (Vowel Buddy phonograms, words, phrases, etc.) to understand how a Vowel Buddy syllable looks. This makes for an easier transition to learning the more complex open and closed syllables. Use SMART (Specific, Measurable, Attainable, Realistic (or Relevant), Timely (Time-bound) goals to assess the progress with syllable types before moving on.

MY NOTES

....

....

....

....

....

CHAPTER 16

SYL-LA-BLE DIVISION
How to Cut the Cake

Wow. We have taken the path beyond sight words and pictures. We have made our way through phonograms, encoding (building), decoding (taking apart), and syllable types. Now, the ability to encounter multisyllabic words and break them down into recognizable parts is the remarkable next step that will radically expand your child's journey to academic and personal growth.

Yes, this is a huge step. But the good news is that you and your child have already done the hard work. Your child:

- Knows the single-letter vowels
- Knows the syllable types

- Knows which vowel sound to choose (because they have learned syllable types)

Since they've done all that, this next step, dividing words into syllables, will have a strong foundation.

Multi-sensory instruction is still the best method. Use your phonogram tiles so you can easily separate and move the syllables.

As usual, we begin with a connection between the familiar and the abstract. Explain that reading words is like eating cake. We do not eat a whole cake in one bite. We cut it up in pieces. Reading an unfamiliar word is just the same. We cut the word into pieces (syllables) until we get through the whole word. Yum!

Sample Clues:

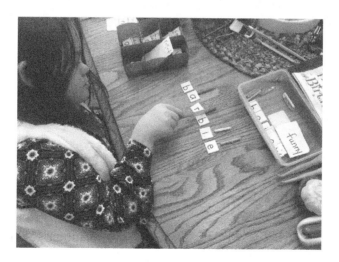

Because this book was developed as an introduction to the concepts of the code, we introduce you to three of the six clues for dividing words into syllables based on the configuration of the vowels and consonants.

Think "portion control" when teaching the following steps. Just as you would not give your child a whole cake to consume in one sitting, you would not want to present them with all these guidelines to consume in one sitting. Let them digest each piece. The verses, as written, are for the adult's benefit. Convey the division guidelines as well as the following steps in your own words to match your child's understanding.

CLUE NUMBER ONE

Here is one of Wordy's clues
to help you to decide:
*cut between two consonants
standing side by side.*

The syllable ends in a consonant;
and if just one vowel is found,
the syllable is closed, and will make a
short vowel sound.

Sample Activity:

Materials:

- Jingle for Clue Number One
- Phonogram Tiles (for specific words)
- Small dry-erase whiteboard
- Dry erase marker
- A two-syllable word list (dinner, happy, happen, rabbit, etc.)
- Birthday candles
- Plastic knife
- For extra fun:
  - horns
  - hats
  - napkins
  - a real cake for an after-activity treat

Demonstrate:
(I Do)

- Using the phonogram tiles, form the word "dinner" on the dry-erase whiteboard
- Underline any multi-letter phonograms (er)
- Place a candle above each vowel. (Explain there are two candles, so we know there are probably two syllables)
- Put your fingers on the two vowel tiles and move them apart (one to the left; one to the right)
- Reposition the candles above the vowels
- Bring attention to the letters between the two vowels
- Name or ask what these letters are called (consonants)
- Sing/say "Cut between two consonants standing side by side" as you cut between the two consonants, moving one to the left and the other to the right to join the other tiles.
- Point to the first syllable and say, "This is a closed syllable. It has one vowel with a consonant at the end. I know this vowel is short and says /ĭ/. (din)
- Point to the second syllable and say, "This is a Bossy R syllable. It has a Bossy R phonogram (er). I know this Bossy R vowel says /er/. (ner)
- "Connect" the two syllables, and pronounce the word while moving your finger from left to right under the connected tiles. (dinner)

Repeat "I do" as needed. During "We do," ask your child questions so they can demonstrate their knowledge. This will show you any necessary further instruction before going on to "You do." If your child is struggling, go back to "We do."

These eleven steps will not occur in one sitting, unless your child has had previous exposure to syllable division. You may focus on "I do" or "We do" for multiple sessions. Take advantage of teachable moments to practice these steps when you are out and about. Menus are a good "worksheet." Apple. Hamburger. Butter. Strawberry.

A fun variation of this exercise is to use plastic plates from a dollar store and write the letters of the word with a dry erase marker on each. Place the plates on the floor, spelling out the word on the floor. Divide the word by sliding the plates (and large candles) left and right. Erase the letters and start over for the next word.

Practice:

After working through the above with several familiar words, begin using nonsense words. This way, your child concentrates on the configuration of letters (vowels and consonants), not on taking hints or reading known words. In this manner, they are demonstrating a true understanding of Clue #1.

Keep data on their progress as you work toward the goal.

MY NOTES

....

....

....

....

....

....

....

....

....

....

....

CLUE NUMBER TWO

When you find one consonant
between two vowel candle flames,
cut after the first vowel.
Make it Open. *Say its name.*

Sample Activity:

Sample words:
diner, fever, donut, remark, final

Directions:

Using Clue #2, follow the same format that you used with Clue Number One.

CLUE NUMBER THREE

But if that word does not make sense
and won't cooperate,
then just behind the consonant
is where you"ll cut the cake.

Sample Activity:

Sample Words:
Visit, robin, talent, camel, river, etc.

Directions:

Introduce Clue #3. Follow all the steps above using two-syllable words that do not follow Clue Number Two. For example, the word "vi-sit" will sound strange, so you exclaim, "That doesn't sound right!" That doesn't make sense. I will try rule #3 and cut _just behind the consonant_." Demonstrate then read the word vis-it correctly. "Now that sounds right! I'll follow Clue Number Three."

A Bonus Tip

Sheet music is a fun way to show and practice syllable division. The words are divided under the notes giving you syllable practice without having to create worksheets. (Hap-py birth-day to you.) You can choose sheets of music, songs in hymnals, or nursery rhymes in music books to point out how words are divided. There are several advantages:

- If children know the songs, they will sing the words and hear the divisions;
- If they don't know the songs, an adult can point to the syllables as they sing;
- Sheet music becomes practice sheets.

TAKEAWAY

Guidelines and examples to show *how* to divide syllables provide a major step in the phonetic journey to independent reading. The bonus is that environmental print, all the words around us, provides the ability to generalize and practice this life-changing information.

MY NOTES

Part Four

MOVING FORWARD with PHONICS the R-IGH-T WAY

In this section, we wish you the best on the path you choose. We say our good-byes, offer you additional information, provide references to learn more about the Science of Reading, and include articles by scientific researchers who study literacy and Down syndrome.

CHAPTER 17

CHOOSING *YOUR* PATH

We hope our explanation of the various components of teaching phonics to individuals with Down syndrome has had an impact and has been valuable to you. We hope, too, that the research findings we have referenced will affirm the hopes and dreams that you have for the great potential of your children and students, of all ages.

We know—from following the research on brain imaging and scientific studies, from the decades of research presented by the Science of Reading, and from our personal experiences—that individuals who are learning to read, from the struggling to the gifted, all benefit from a foundation in phonics. However, our mission with this book is to raise the expectations and knowledge of those who specifically love and work with individuals who have Down syndrome.

If we can save even a few parents the years of heartache that Judy went through or any child the years of failure Casey experienced, we will have fulfilled our mission. If we can convince even a few hesitant professionals that their students do have the potential to read independently when given the proper instruction, we will have further fulfilled our mission.

The full path that ventures beyond the ABCs and sight words is, admittedly, not a short, stressless stroll through a sunflower garden. You may wend your way sometimes with impatience, sometimes frustration, sometimes doubt. But these are not new feelings for you. We have yet to meet the parent or the professional who constantly experiences confidence and conviction. However difficult this may be at times, we know you will also encounter dreams materialized, hopes renewed, and joys shared.

As we have indicated earlier, current research, and that going back decades, has provided the data that prove phonics is the most effective method. The list in our Afterword is just a beginning.

Now you have discovered (or been reminded of) this direction. We hope you take these first steps and continue to bring your own experiences, knowledge, and devotion to make the next pathway your own. We remind you, as well, that phonics is just the beginning of real reading. It forms the foundation for comprehension and true enjoyment of discovering new things through rich literature. All of these can happen simultaneously when you add comprehension strategies and share meaningful literature, both fiction and non-fiction with your loved one.

We have helped you discover this path to reading. Now you can make it *yours*. Know that there are guides to help you.

Take your child's hand and lead the way. This is where your child or student will find *their* personal path—the one that leads first to reading, then to the myriad people, places, and opportunities they would otherwise never have discovered.

Thank you for joining us. Our best wishes go with each of you and your children.

We would love to hear from you.

Blessings,
Judy and Marilee

If we can help, let us know.

info@PhonicsTheRightWay.com
info@RaisingRobustReaders.com

Useful Definitions

USEFUL DEFINITIONS

SPOKEN LANGUAGE TERMS
Phon—hear   ology—the study of

PHONICS is a method of teaching people to read based on the sounds that letters represent.

PHONEMES are the smallest parts of sound in spoken words. For instance, there are three sounds in the spoken word cat /k/ /ă/ /t/. There are also three sounds in the spoken word caught /k/ /aw/ /t/, even though that word has six letters. Generally, we recognize forty-four sounds in the English language. Please note that when you see letters within slash marks //, you pronounce the sound, not the name, of the letter.

PHONEMIC AWARENESS is the ability to identify and manipulate individual sounds in spoken words. "Bat" begins with the initial sound /b/. "Tab" ends with the final sound /b/. Being able to move sounds and decode the words indicates skill in phonemic awareness.

PHONOLOGICAL AWARENESS is a broader term that includes phonemic awareness. It, too, refers to spoken words, but it also includes identifying and manipulating larger parts of spoken language, such as syllables and sentences.

WRITTEN LANGUAGE TERMS
gram; graph—written

LETTERS, in general, refers to the twenty-six symbols that make up the English language. They can also combine to create multi-letter phonograms, such as "ay" or "eigh."

PHONOGRAMS are single letters (the alphabet) and two (oa)-, three (igh)-, and four-letter (augh) combinations that show just one sound. For instance, the single-letter phonogram "f" represents the sound /f/, and the two-letter phonogram "ph" also represents the sound /f/. Generally recognized, there are seventy-two basic phonograms in English.

GRAPHEMES are written symbols that represent a sound (phoneme). This can be a single letter or a combination of letters, as noted above. When we say the sound /p/, this is a phoneme; but when we write the letter "p," it is a grapheme.

ORTHOGRAPHIC refers to that part of language that involves letters and spelling.

APPENDIX B

72 Phonograms

 The 72 Phonograms
Phonograms Show the Smallest Sounds We Read.

Alphabet Phonograms

a_3 b c_2 d e_2 f g_2 h i_3 j k l m
n o_3 p qu r s_2 t u_3 v w x_2 y_4 z

Vowel Buddy Phonograms

ai ay eigh ee igh oa oe
er ur ir ear ar_3 or_2 au aw augh oi oy
ea_3 ei_2 ey_2 ie_2 ew_2 ue_2 ui_2 ow_2 oo_3 ou_4 $ough_6$

Consonant Partner Phonograms

tch sh wh ng ph ck gn kn wr mb dge
th_2 ch_3 ed_3 ci ti si_2

© 2020 Raising Robust Readers

Phonemic Awareness Games

PHONEMIC AWARENESS GAMES

The ability to hear, say, and manipulate sounds (phonemic awareness) is one of the greatest predictors of reading success. It is important that we give children ample opportunity to learn and practice this skill. It is one of the most beneficial areas upon which to concentrate in early literacy instruction.

Picture Cards (beginning sounds)
Place pictures on a table and ask your child to find a picture that starts with the sound of /__/.

Draw from a deck of picture cards and identify the first sound of the picture.

Clapping Games (syllable awareness)
Have children clap the number of syllables in names. Music is especially useful to clap syllables. Each beat is a syllable and can be easily identified and clapped out.

Play "Take the Sound Away" (deleting sounds and syllables)
Say the word (example: "baseball.") Repeat—only this time leave out either the beginning or ending of the word (Example: "base___" or "___ball." Ask your child what you took away. Start with compound words, then move to multi-syllable words. Continue the game until you are successfully dropping the beginning and ending sounds of

one-syllable words. Reverse the game and have your child ask you to identify sounds that he/she takes away.

Compound Words

> football
> railroad
> upside
> today
> toothpaste

Multi-Syllable Words

> little
> happy
> sofa
> hamburger
> peanut

One-Syllable Words

> rain
> hat
> bay
> hand
> car

Alphabet Phonogram Pronunciation Guide

Sound-Pronunciation Guide

Alphabet Phonograms

Alphabet Phonograms Sound-Symbol Pronunciation Guide

Comment: We do not add an 'uh' sound to the end of the phonogram, especially /b/. Concentrate on puffing out air and eliminating the 'uh' sound. Think of the word 'big.' Say it to yourself. Now just pronounce the /b/ without the 'ig.'

Single-Sound Consonants

Phonogram	Sound Symbol	Example
b	/b/	big
d	/d/	dig
f	/f/	fan
h	/h/	hat
j	/j/	jump
k	/k/	kick
l	/l/	left
m	/m/	march
n	/n/	no
p	/p/	picture
qu	/kw/	quit
r	/r/	right
t	/t/	tap
v	/v/	van
w	/w/	window
z	/z/	zip

Two-Sound Consonants

Phonogram	Sound Symbol	Example
c	/k/ /s/	cut / center
g	/g/ /j/	gate / gerbil
s	/s/ /z/	snake / flies
x	/ks/ /z/	box / xylophone

Multi-Sound Vowels

Phonogram	Sound Symbol	Example
a	/ă/ /ā/ /ah/	Abby / ate / almonds
e	/ĕ/ /ē/	egg / me
i	/ĭ/ /ī/ /ē/	hit / like / champion
o	/ŏ/ /ō/ /oō/	hop / go / into
u	/ŭ/ /ū/ /oŏ/	up / use / put
y	/y/ /ē/ /ī/ /ĭ/	yellow / noisy / my / cymbals

Vowel Partner Phonogram Guide

Sound-Pronunciation Guide
Vowel-Partner Phonograms

Sound Symbol Pronunciation Guide
Vowel Buddy Phonograms

Phonogram	Sound Symbol	Example
ai	/ā/	sail
ay	/ā/	ray
eigh	/ā/	eight
ee	/ē/	see
igh	/ī/	high
oa	/ō/	boat
oe	/ō/	toe

Phonogram	Sound Symbol	Example
oi	/oy/	join
oy	/oy/	toy
au	/aw/	autograph
aw	/aw/	draw
augh	/aw/	taught

Phonogram	Sound Symbol	Example
ea	/ē/ /ĕ/ /ā/	eat / bread / steak
ei	/ē/ /ā/	weird/ beige
ey	/ē/ /ā/	key / say
ie	/ē/ /ī/	piece / pie

Phonogram	Sound Symbol	Example
ew	/oō/ /ū/	flew / view
ue	/oō/ /ū/	blue / argue
ui	/oō/ /ī/	juice / biscuit

Phonogram	Sound Symbol	Example
ow	/ow/ /ō/	bow / low
oo	/oō/ /oŏ/ /ō/	room / wood / door
ou	/ow/ /oō/ /ŭ/ /ō/	ouch / you / touch / shoulder
ough	/aw/ /ō/ /ŭf/ /off/ /ow/ /oō/	thought / although / rough cough / plough / through

Bossy R and Consonant-Partner Pronunciation Guide

Sound-Pronunciation Guide
Bossy R and Consonant-Partner Phonograms

Sound Symbol Pronunciation Guide
Bossy r Phonograms and Consonant Partner Phonograms

Bossy r Phonograms

Phonogram	Sound Symbol	Example
er	/er/	hiker
ur	/er/	hurt
ir	/er/	dirt
ear	/er/	earth
or	/or/ /er/	orange / color
ar	/ar/ /er/ /or/	car / backward/ warn

Phonogram	Sound Symbol	Example
tch	/ch/	scratch
sh	/sh/	shy
wh	/wh/	when
ng	/ng/	sing
ph	/f/	phone
ck	/k/	sick
gn	/n/	gnaw
kn	/n/	knee
wr	/r/	wrap
mb	/m/	climb
dge	/j/	fudge

Phonogram	Sound Symbol	Example
th	/th/ tz/	three / those
ch	/ch/ /k/ /sh/	chest / stomach/ mustache
ed	/ed/ /d/ /t/	pounded / rubbed / wiped

Phonogram	Sound Symbol	Example
ci	/sh/	magician
ti	/sh/	demonstration
si	/sh/ /zh/	suspension / illusion

Short Assessment Chart

Initial-Phonogram-Assessment Chart

		name	sound	name	sound
Phonogram Assessment Chart		— B —	— b —
		— D —	— d —
Name_____		— F —	— f —
		— H —	— h —
Date_____		— J —	— j —
		— K —	— k —
	+ knows the sound	— L —	— l —
	✓ needs refinement	— M —	— m —
	• hesitates	— N —	— n —
	--does not know	— P —	— p —
		— Qu —	— qu —
Bonus phonograms:		— R —	— r —
		— T —	— t —
		— V —	— v —
ai ___	er ___	— W —	— w —
ay ___	ur ___	— Z —	— z —
eigh ___	ir ___		
ee ___	ear ___		
igh ___	or ___ ___	— C ___ ___	— c ___ ___
oa ___	ar ___ ___ ___	— G ___ ___	— g ___ ___
oe ___		— S ___ ___	— s ___ ___
		— X ___ ___	— x ___ ___
This student also knows:			
		— Y ___ ___ ___ ___	— y ___ ___ ___ ___
___ ___ ___ ___			
Comments:		— A ___ ___ ___	— a ___ ___ ___
		— E ___ ___	— e ___ ___
		— I ___ ___ ___ ___	— i ___ ___ ___ ___
		— O ___ ___ ___	— o ___ ___ ___
		— U ___ ___ ___	— u ___ ___ ___

Complete Assessment Chart

Complete-Phonogram-Assessment Chart

| **Phonogram Assessment Chart** |

- [ ] a _ _ _
- [ ] b
- [ ] c _ _
- [ ] d
- [ ] e _ _
- [ ] f
- [ ] g _ _
- [ ] h
- [ ] i _ _ _
- [ ] j
- [ ] k
- [ ] l
- [ ] m
- [ ] n
- [ ] o_ _ _
- [ ] p
- [ ] q_u
- [ ] r
- [ ] s _ _
- [ ] t
- [ ] u _ _ _
- [ ] v
- [ ] w
- [ ] x _ _
- [ ] y _ _ _ _
- [ ] z

- [ ] tch
- [ ] sh
- [ ] wh
- [ ] ng
- [ ] ph
- [ ] ck
- [ ] gn
- [ ] kn
- [ ] wr
- [ ] mb
- [ ] dge
- [ ] th _ _
- [ ] ch _ _ _
- [ ] ed _ _ _
- [ ] ti
- [ ] ci
- [ ] si _ _
- [ ] er
- [ ] ur
- [ ] ir
- [ ] ear
- [ ] ar _ _ _
- [ ] or _ _

- [ ] ai
- [ ] ay
- [ ] eigh
- [ ] ee
- [ ] igh
- [ ] oa
- [ ] oe
- [ ] au
- [ ] aw
- [ ] augh
- [ ] oi
- [ ] oy
- [ ] ea _ _ _
- [ ] ei _ _
- [ ] ey _ _
- [ ] ie _ _
- [ ] ew_ _
- [ ] ue _ _
- [ ] ui _ _
- [ ] ow _ _
- [ ] oo _ _ _
- [ ] ou _ _ _ _
- [ ] ough _ _ _ _ _ _

Name_____

Date _____

SOUNDS
Mark on the right

+ knows the sound
✓ needs refinement
• hesitates
— does not know

COMMENTS:

How to Teach a Phonogram

HOW TO TEACH A PHONOGRAM

Six Steps to Success

HEAR It - SEE It   MOVE It   PLAY

FIND IT   MATCH IT   WRITE It - Yeah!

Phonogram "ay" Page

ay

'a-y' makes an /ā/.
'a-y' makes an /ā/.
I see a ray in the bay.
'a-y' makes an /ā/.

Vowel Buddy Word List

Vowel Buddy Word List
ai, ay, eigh, ee, igh, oa, oe

ai	ay	eigh	ee		igh	oa	oe
aid			bee	queer	high	oaf	doe
ail	bay	eight	beep	reef	light	oak	foe
aim	day	neigh	beef	reek	might	oar	hoe
air	Fay	weigh	beet	reel	fight	oat	Joe
bail	hay	weight	Dee	tee	night	boat	Joel
bait	jay		deed	teem	right	boar	Moe
fail	Jay		deep	teen	tight	foal	Noel
fair	Kay		deer	veer		foam	poem
hail	lay		eek	wee		Joan	roe
hair	may		eel	weed	sigh	load	toe
jail	May		fee	week	sight	loaf	woe
laid	nay		feed	weep		loam	
lain	pay		feel			loan	
lair	ray		feet	gee		moan	
maid	Ray		heed	geek		moat	
mail	way		heel	see		road	
main			jeep	seed		roam	
nail			jeer	seek		roan	
paid			keel	seem		toad	
pail	cay		keen	seen			
pain	gay		keep	seep		coat	
pair	say		lee	seer		goad	
quail			leek			goat	
raid			leer			soak	
rail			meek			soap	
rain			meet				
tail			need				
waif			peek				
wail			peel				
wait			peep				
gain			peer				
gait			queen				
sail							

Note: Some of these words may be advanced vocabulary for your child. The object is to be able to blend sounds together. Your child does not have to understand all the words. But do not miss the opportunity to expand his or her vocabulary. Underline the sail-away phonograms when writing them. Eventually fade this step.

©2023 Raising Robust Readers

Phonogram Tile Kit

Phonogram Tile Kit. It is important for students to learn how vowel sounds interact with consonant sounds to make words. Separating these sounds into categories is an important first step. This folder will create a great visual and interactive activity to help students see and learn the difference between consonant and vowel sounds. In addition, these tiles can be used for word building and assessments. Download color-coded kit from www.RaisingRobustReaders.com

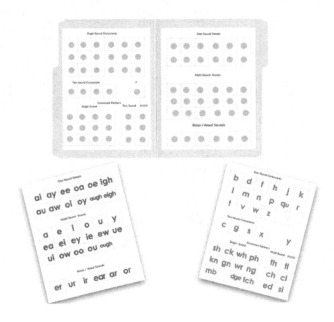

Part Five

SUPPORTING PHONICS

"Come with the facts.
Emotion is not going to get you anywhere."

(Before every IEP)
Roger O'Halloran, Attorney,
Casey's dad

AFTERWORD

RESOURCES and RESEARCH
Don't Take Just Our Word for It

Check our website under RESOURCES at RaisingRobustReaders.com. for more information.

OUR FAVORITES

Facebook Group Page: Phonics for Folks with Down Syndrome. Admittedly, recommending this page created by Raising Robust Readers™ may seem self-serving. But it is actually member-serving. Families and professionals join to learn and share practical information and experiences. It is a community of members who care about their children and their students with Down syndrome and want the best for them. https://www.facebook.com/groups/629246527654149/

Reading Rockets is *our five-star recommendation* as a one-stop shop for gaining information on all aspects of reading. Simplified summaries on the scholarly articles are a real plus. But, then again, everything they produce is a real plus. Their website description reads, "Reading Rockets is a national multimedia project that offers a wealth of research-based reading strategies, lessons, and activities designed to help young children learn how to read and read better. Our reading resources assist parents, teachers, and other educators in helping struggling readers build fluency, vocabulary, and comprehension skills." (readingrockets.org)

Emily Hanford, Senior Education Correspondent with America Public Media. Since 2017, Emily has produced a series of podcasts that bring to light the woeful state of reading scores, the reasons, and some important solutions. She has accomplished what researchers and neuroscientists have not been able to: she has reached the general public (and educators) on a large scale basis to enlighten and change.

Dr. Stanislas Dehaene is a leading cognitive neuroscientist and winner of the 2014 Grete Lundbeck European Brain Research Prize. Professor Dehaene has led the field in showing how the brain learns to read. His MRI brain images and explanations are real game-changers in proving why phonemic awareness and phonics are necessary for effective reading.

Start with: https://www.youtube.com/watch?v=25GI3-kiLdo

Bruce McCandliss, PhD, is the head of the Educational Neuroscience Initiative at Stanford University, doing research on academic neuroscience and education. His research using MRI supports shows that sounding out words sparks more brain activity than memorizing words. https://ed.stanford.edu/faculty/brucemc and https://ed.stanford.edu/news/stanford-brain-wave-study-shows-how-different-teaching-methods-affect-reading-development.

Christopher Lemons, PhD, is a Professor at the College of Education, Stanford University. Along with his many research articles, he conveys a positive and encouraging attitude about the abilities of students with intellectual disabilities. https://ed.stanford.edu/faculty/cjlemons and https://ed.stanford.edu/news/stanford-program-equips-paraeducators-work-more-effectively-disabled-students.

The Reading League. The Reading League's mission is to demystify the science of reading so that more educators become aware of it, understand it, and use it to cultivate strong readers. Primarily aimed at teaching professionals, the League has valuable information for parents as well. https://www.thereadingleague.org/

"The Great Reading Rethink" in the August 2022 issue of Time Magazine is a compelling fact-filled article highlighted with personal stories from families, teachers, and administrators. Luscombe, Belinda. "The Great Reading Rethink." *Time*, Aug. 2022, pp. 63–67. https://time.com/6205084/phonics-science-of-reading-teachers/

YOUTUBE

YouTube is a valuable source of information. We can combine listening, reading (slides, captions, etc.) plus the added bonus of being able to pause, rewind, and replay when it benefits us. We caution our readers to be critical listeners when they are searching for videos. Critical - not in the vein of finding fault, but critical in the vein of listening carefully and evaluating the reliability of the information.

Raising Robust Readers Channel - Down syndrome Playlist - https://www.youtube.com/playlist?list=PLVg58gSFrdxwINSuCsQJ8qtrxalHVclVC

Dr. Stanislas Dehaene - fascinating videos of his work with brain imaging.

Lecture by Dr. Stanislas Dehaene on "Reading the Brain" - https://www.youtube.com/watch?v=MSy685vNqYk

Bruce McCandliss: "Brain mechanisms of early reading skills" Presentation at Johns Hopkins, February 2016.
Bruce McCandliss: "Brain mechanisms of early reading skills"

Michelle Elia - is one of two Literacy Leads with the Ohio Department of Education. Her presentations 'translate' the science of reading, brain research, and differentiated instruction into easy-to-understand presentations. https://www.youtube.com/watch?v=-BPpkJOyMAI&t=3s

Brett Stephens: hosts the Podcast - Science of Reading Special Education - Interview with Judy O'Halloran Teaching Children with Down syndrome, Autism, and Cognitive Challenges to Read https://www.youtube.com/watch?v=XaLvk_X6hLk&t=355s

ESTABLISHED BY CONGRESS

NRP - National Reading Panel

In 1997, Congress convened the National Reading Panel under the National Institutes of Health. The panel was made up of 14 people, including leading scientists in reading research, college representatives, teachers, educational administrators, and parents. The stated aim of the Panel was to assess the effectiveness of different approaches used to teach children to read. On April 13, 2000, the panel concluded its work and submitted its reports which identified five key components for effective reading instruction: Phonemic Awareness, Phonics, Fluency, Vocabulary, and Comprehension. https://www.nichd.nih.gov/research/supported/nrp

NAEP - The National Assessment of Educational Progress (NAEP), often called **The Nation's Report Card**, (NRC) is a congressionally mandated large-scale assessment administered by the National Center for Education Statistics (NCES). It assesses students in public and private schools to determine what they know and are able to do in various subjects. The 2022 report, as well as previous reports, reveals that two-thirds of 4th and 8th graders read below proficiency." https://nces.ed.gov/nationsreportcard/reading/

ADVOCACY—KNOW YOUR CHILD'S RIGHTS

Department of Education, Office of Special Education Programs
https://www2.ed.gov/about/offices/list/osers/osep/about.html

"The mission of the Office of Special Education Programs (OSEP) is to lead the nation's efforts to improve outcomes for children with disabilities, birth through 21, and their families, ensuring access to fair, equitable, and high-quality education and services. Our vision is for a world in which individuals with disabilities have unlimited opportunities to learn and to lead purposeful and fulfilling lives."

Individuals with Disabilities Education Act (IDEA)
https://sites.ed.gov/idea/

"IDEA is a federal law that makes available a free appropriate public education to eligible children with disabilities and ensures special education and related services to those children who qualify. It governs how states and public agencies provide early intervention, special education, and related services to eligible infants, toddlers, children, and youth with disabilities."

Wright's Law
https://www.wrightslaw.com/

"Wrightslaw provides free access to articles, legal cases, training, and resources about special education law and advocacy."

Parents for Reading Justice

Brett Tingley, President, explains how a parent movement began and spread to address the needs of struggling readers with dyslexia. (parentsforreadingjustice.org) Watch her moving introduction here: https://www.youtube.com/watch?v=Hi7ep3wFa1A&t=39s

We hope the takeaway from this video is that parents realize they can lead the movement to be sure our students with Down syndrome receive instruction in Science of Reading methodology and that they are not left out of the best practices for teaching reading.

NATIONAL DOWN SYNDROME ORGANIZATIONS

GiGi's Playhouse Down Syndrome Achievement Centers

The nationwide locations provide free educational, therapeutic-based, and career development programs for individuals with Down syndrome, their families, and the community.

We are pleased to partner with GiGi's Playhouse Down Syndrome Achievement Centers to incorporate phonics into their literacy sessions.

Down Syndrome Resource Foundation

The DSRF supports people in Canada living with Down syndrome and their families "with individualized and leading-edge educational programs, health services, information resources." Their website information on reading, not just for Canadians, is definitely leading-edge. https://www.dsrf.org/resources/information/education/reading/

MY NOTES

....
....
....
....
....
....
....

IN SHORT...

Bazin-Berryman, Mireille. Reading: Children with Down Syndrome BU Journal of Graduate Studies in Education, Volume 10, Issue 2, 2018

Children with Down syndrome have a relative strength in word recognition because of their visual memory strength. There has been a pattern of using only the whole-word approach to teach reading to children with Down syndrome (Baylis & Snowling, 2012), but we should not limit their learning by offering only one strategy (Cologon, 2013). Phonological awareness training can make a difference for reading progress in children with Down syndrome (Baylis & Snowling, 2012), particularly in word recognition and decoding skills (Mengoni, Nash, & Hulme, 2014).

In conclusion, word recognition, phonological awareness, orthographic knowledge, and reading comprehension must specifically be taught to all children, but in particular to children with Down syndrome in a way that is conducive to their reading and learning profile. Teacher education must include the different ways to intervene in reading for children with Down syndrome because of the prevalence of these children in our regular stream classrooms. Successfully teaching children with Down syndrome to read provides them an effective mode of communication, which in turn supports their inclusion in society, their contribution to society, and their autonomy.

Dehaene, Stanislas.2022. "The Massive Impact of Literacy on the Brain and its Consequences for Education." Human Neuroplasticity and Education. 19-32. https://www.unicog.org/publications/Dehaene%20 Review%20Cognitive%20neuroscience%20of%20Reading%20and%20 Education%202011.pdf

The current thinking is that, during reading of a single word, millions of hierarchically organized neurons, each tuned to a specific local property (a letter, a bigram, or a morpheme), collectively contribute to visual recognition. This massively parallel architecture explains the speed and robustness of visual word recognition. Most importantly, for educators and teachers, it creates an illusion of whole-word reading. Because reading is so fast and takes about the same time for short and long words, some have assumed that the overall whole-word shape is being used for recognition, and that we should therefore teach whole-word reading rather than by letter-to-sound decoding. This inference is wrong, however.

MY NOTES

....

....

....

....

....

....

....

....

....

....

....

REFERENCES

Allor, Jill H., Patricia G. Mathes, J. Kyle Roberts, Jennifer P. Cheatham, and Tammi M. Champlin. May, 2010. "Comprehensive Reading Instruction for Students with Intellectual Disabilities: Findings From the First Three Years of a Longitudinal Study" Psychology in the Schools. 47 (5):445-466

Baltagu, Ibragun. "How Music Affects Your Baby's Brain: Mini Parenting Master Class." n.d. Www.unicef.org. https://www.unicef.org/parenting/child-development/how-music-affects-your-babys-brain-class

Baylis, Pamela, and Margaret J Snowling. 2012. "Evaluation of a Phonological Reading Programme for Children with Down Syndrome." Child Language Teaching and Therapy 28 (1): 39–56.

Cologon, Kathy. 2013. "Debunking Myths: Reading Development in Children with Down Syndrome." Australian Journal of Teacher Education 38 (3).

Hale, Natalie. 2023. Whole Child Reading: A Quick-Start Guide to Teaching Students with Down Syndrome and Other Developmental Delays. Special Reads for Special Needs.

Laws, Glynis, Heather Brown, and Elizabeth Main. 2015. "Reading Comprehension in Children with Down Syndrome." Reading and Writing 29 (1): 21–45.

Lemons, Christopher J. Supporting Literacy and Inclusion for Students with Intellectual and Developmental Disabilities, September 11, 2022. https://az659834.vo.msecnd.net/eventsairaueprod/production-gems-public/884abe1668ec4378b692984ec42547b4.

Lemons, Christopher J., Jill H. Allor, Stephanie Al Otaiba, and Lauren M. LeJeune. 2016. "10 Research-Based Tips for Enhancing Literacy Instruction for

Students with Intellectual Disability." TEACHING Exceptional Children 49 (1): 18–30.

Lyon, G. Reid. 1999. "Reading Development, Reading Disorders, and Reading Instruction: Research-Based Findings." Perspectives on Language Learning and Education 6 (1): 8–16.

McGuinness, Diane. 2006. Early Reading Instruction. MIT Press.

Mengoni, Silvana E., Hanna M. Nash, and Charles Hulme. 2012. "The Benefit of Orthographic Support for Oral Vocabulary Learning in Children with Down Syndrome." Journal of Child Language 40 (1): 221–43.

Mengoni, Silvana E., Hanna M. Nash, and Charles Hulme. 2014. "Learning to Read New Words in Individuals with Down Syndrome: Testing the Role of Phonological Knowledge." Research in Developmental Disabilities 35 (5): 1098–1109.

Moats. Louisa Cook. 2004. LETRS, Language Essentials for Teachers of Reading and Spelling. Book 2, Modules 4, 5, 6. Longmont, Co.: Sopris West Educational Services.

Næss, Kari-Anne B., Monica Melby-Lervåg, Charles Hulme, and Solveig-Alma Halaas Lyster. 2012. "Reading Skills in Children with Down Syndrome: A Meta-Analytic Review." Research in Developmental Disabilities 33 (2): 737–47.

Roch, Maja, and M. Chiara Levorato. 2009. "Simple View of Reading in Down's Syndrome: The Role of Listening Comprehension and Reading Skills." International Journal of Language & Communication Disorders 44 (2): 206–23.

Sermier Dessemontet, Rachel, Catherine Martinet, Anne-Françoise de Chambrier, Britt-Marie Martini-Willemin, and Catherine Audrin. 2019. "A Meta-Analysis on the Effectiveness of Phonics Instruction for Teaching Decoding Skills to Students with Intellectual Disability." Educational Research Review 26 (February): 52–70.

Sermier Dessemontet, Rachel, and Anne-Françoise de Chambrier. 2015. "The Role of Phonological Awareness and Letter-Sound Knowledge in the Reading

Development of Children with Intellectual Disabilities." Research in Developmental Disabilities 41-42 (June): 1–12.

Stockard, Jean, Timothy W. Wood, Cristy Coughlin, and Caitlin Rasplica Khoury. 2018. "The Effectiveness of Direct Instruction Curricula: A Meta-Analysis of a Half Century of Research." Review of Educational Research 88 (4): 479–507.

Wong, May. 2015. Review of Stanford Study on Brain Waves Shows How Different Teaching Methods Affect Reading Development. Stanford News, May.

MY NOTES

ABOUT THE AUTHORS

JUDY O'HALLORAN

A nationally-recognized program developer, author, educator, and speaker, Judy's advocacy and actions are inspired by her son Casey who has Down syndrome. Judy brings to parents and educators an uplifting spirit of high expectations and practical skills for their children and adults with Down syndrome. She lives the adage, "If you're not a part of the solution, you're a part of the problem." Her hope is that *Phonics the R-igh-t Way* will be part of the solution in giving our children and students, of all ages, the skills to reach their individual potential to read independently. O'Halloran and her husband, Roger, live in Fort Myers, Florida, and enjoy having their three sons, three daughters-in-law, and five grandchildren nearby. Judy is especially grateful that Roger took up cooking just before she started this book.

MARILEE SENIOR

Marilee Senior is a founding partner of Raising Robust Readers™ and has spent the past twenty years studying the science of reading. Along with Judy O'Halloran, she co-wrote *The ABCs of the Sounds We Read*, a 2015 Moonbeam Children's Book Award winner. Together they developed the internationally-used Raising Robust Readers™ 18-module Reading Program. A creative artist, Senior's graphics throughout their website and books add enjoyment and clarity. Senior graduated from Florida SouthWestern State College and furthered her studies at the

University of Houston. Her personal struggle with dyslexia and her love of Judy O'Halloran's son, Casey, inspire her quest to offer child-centered reading instruction to as many people as possible, but especially those with Down syndrome.

If you enjoyed this book, please take a few moments to write a review. Help others discover the path to independent reading.
Thank You,
Judy and Marilee

Made in the USA
Monee, IL
25 July 2024

61916336R00125